First Lady of the Seeing Eye

Books by Blake Clark:

Oriental England

Omai, First Polynesian Ambassador to England

Paradise, Unlimited

Remember Pearl Harbor

Advertising Smoke Screen

Robinson Crusoe, USN

Into Siam (with Nicol Smith)

Hawaii, Forty-ninth State

First Lady
of the
Seeing Eye

by

MORRIS FRANK

and

BLAKE CLARK

Holt, Rinehart and Winston
New York · Chicago · San Francisco

In Canada, Holt, Rinehart
and Winston of Canada, Limited
Library of Congress Catalog Card Number: 57-7356

Published, April, 1957
Second Printing, October, 1957
Third Printing, October, 1958
Fourth Printing, November, 1962

82920–0117

Printed in the United States of America

To my friends who made life worth
living and The Seeing Eye possible,
and to Mrs. Wonderful, Lois, my wife

Acknowledgments

The authors thank The Seeing Eye of Morristown, New Jersey, for their cooperation, and Deena Clark for her professional contribution to the organizing, editing, and writing of this book.

January, 1957

MORRIS FRANK
BLAKE CLARK

First Lady of the Seeing Eye

Chapter 1

ᴄ─ᴄ─ᴄ─ᴄ─ᴄ─ᴄ─ᴄ

PERHAPS the closest brush I have ever had with death came in a hotel corridor in Dayton, Ohio. The near-disaster occurred because I am blind. But it need not have happened at all; and it was solely my own fault.

I was scheduled to address a large convention in Dayton that evening, the train had arrived late and I was pressed for time. With Buddy, the Seeing Eye guide dog who served as my eyes, I rushed up to my room on the fourteenth floor. After I had freshened up I had only fifteen minutes to get to the convention hall. I had to hurry downstairs and find a cab.

With my ever-present German shepherd companion I hustled along the corridor to the elevator foyer. There Buddy stopped stock-still. She, who always walked up to an elevator and pointed with her nose to the call button for my convenience, would not approach this one. She ignored completely my "Forward" command. Then, in my great haste, I did what no Seeing Eye owner should ever do—I dropped the harness and started forward alone.

Buddy immediately threw herself across my legs, pushing so hard against me that I could not move ahead. At that moment a maid coming out of one of the rooms let out a terrified shriek.

"Don't move!" she shouted. "The elevator door's open, but the elevator's not there! There's only a hole!"

11

My knees all but buckled. Had Buddy let me take two more steps I would have disappeared down the empty shaft!

In that grateful and revealing instant there flashed through my mind an acute realization of just how much the loyalty and intelligence of that beautiful German shepherd lady had meant to me. And not only to me, but to all of the American blind who had secured freedom and independence through the use of trained guide dogs. For Buddy was the first Seeing Eye dog in America—the pioneer who opened the way for all the others. All her actions were attended by the widest publicity, and were watched with a curiosity which was at first profoundly skeptical. Had her performance not been brilliant and flawless, it is quite possible that the Seeing Eye program would never have got under way in America.

A few years earlier I had never heard of trained guide dogs for the blind. Then one day—I vividly remember the date, November 5, 1927—I was downtown in Nashville, Tennessee, where I was born and raised.

A brisk breeze laden with cold moisture from the Cumberland River chilled me as my attendant led me from my bank on Union Street. I pulled my topcoat collar up around my chin and then haltingly felt my way with my cane for the curb. I sensed my nearness to the corner newsstand. Charlie, the crippled vendor, shouted out to me, "Hey, Mr. Frank, there's a piece in this week's *Post* you oughta read! It's about blind folks like you."

I felt in my pocket for a nickel and handed it up. That five cents bought an article that was worth more than a million dollars to me. It changed my whole life.

That night—November 5, 1927—while I sat in the living room of our home on Richland Avenue, my father read those important words aloud. "This is called *The Seeing Eye,*" he began, his voice husky with emotion.

In the article, the author, Dorothy Harrison Eustis, described how the Germans had trained shepherd dogs to take the place of a blind man's eyes. I listened with mounting excitement as Father read that these marvelous dogs were equipped with a special harness, a firm, croquet-wicket-shaped leather handle that became a vital link between themselves and their masters. That short piece of leather was literally a lifeline. Through it the dog communicated as clearly and unhesitatingly as if he had been able to speak the words: "Straight ahead, path's clear"; "Slow down, sidewalk crowded"; or "Stop! Dangerous intersection!"

A dog would lead his charge at a fast walk so that any slackening of the gait could be instantly felt through the rigid handle. The miracle of it was that the animal could not only warn that the path ahead was not clear, he could even indicate what hazard was obstructing it. For curbs, he pulled back and stood still so his master could find the edge with his foot; for a bank of steps, he sat down; for busy traffic intersections, he "froze" until it was safe to cross. He swerved to either right or left to avoid stationary objects like scaffoldings and letter boxes, and he dodged oncoming pedestrians with uncanny agility.

As I listened, I could hardly control the wild hope that rose in me. If what we read about these wonder-working dogs was really true, they could free a person from the worst and most humiliating part of being blind—one's continual, helpless dependence on others. A companionable dog could take the place of an impatient human attendant, or—what was worse—a pitying one.

A dog's gentle pull could take me safely around open manholes, sidewalk-parked baby carriages, or the stray tricycles that were ever-present booby traps on even my simplest ventures outside the house. He could be my own personal red and green light at harrowing street crossings, sympathetically protecting me from potentially death-dealing tons of glass and steel on wheels.

My father paused in his reading. My mother, realizing what this revelation could mean to all of us, wordlessly sat down beside me. The promise held out seemed too good to be true.

The author herself told of her first skepticism. How could a dog be trained to do all that was claimed? An experience then at the Potsdam training school convinced her.

She followed a blind man who set off with his guide dog, bound for the public gardens over a mile away. They safely negotiated city streets crowded with pedestrians. They crossed intersections alive with darting little automobiles, three-wheeled dog carts, and roaring motorcycles. So far, so good, but after all, the dog had successfully avoided only the *usual* type of hazard. Then the man and his four-footed guide approached one of those waist-high iron railings put up to keep cyclists off the sidewalk. Would the dog do the natural thing for her and simply trot on under the bar? If she did, the blind man would collide full force with the barrier for quite a blow right in his middle. Mrs. Eustis watched with a catch in her throat as she saw the dog, despite having to skirt a discarded coat on the ground, make for the narrow opening provided for pedestrians, and dog and master wheeled safely into the sunshine-filled, green park.

The future of all blind could be the same, the article promised. No longer dependent upon a member of the family, a friend, or a paid attendant, they could once more take up normal lives almost where they had been cut off. Each could begin or go back to a wage-earning occupation, secure in the knowledge that he could get to and from his work safely and without the cost of a hired guide; that crowds and traffic need no longer hold any terrors for him. His self-respect would be restored. After an honest day's work his evenings could be spent among friends without responsibility or burden to them;

he need no longer be led home like a child—an ignominy
that erased the whole pleasure of the visit.

"Gentlemen," the author concluded, "again without reservation, I give you the shepherd dog."

There was a choke in my father's voice as he finished. We
sat silent for a moment, then all began talking at once. Our
words overlapped, knocked into one another as flint against
flint, ignited and lighted a once gloomy room with the blessed
brightness of hope. After that evening, life was never the same
for any of us.

I tossed and turned all night. One of these extraordinary
animals could be the answer to my prayers. He could ease the
bitterness I felt at losing my sight. By a series of coincidences
—so rare that I wonder whether it ever happened to another
family—my mother and I were both blinded accidentally, at
times years apart, and each of us lost one eye at a time. Mother
lost the first after a blood vessel in it burst while she was under
strain of childbirth; a fall from a horse caused the loss of the
second.

I lost my right eye at six when I ran into a tree limb while
riding horseback. Then, at sixteen, came an unfortunate blow
during a boxing match and within two days I saw no more.
Now, after four years of blindness, the thought of the guide
dogs opened vistas I had feared forever closed to me.

I visualized myself walking freely down the street. I would
be able to make calls on prospective clients for my insurance
business without the encumbrance of a talkative, incompati-
ble guide. I could go to college on my own. I could even have
a date—and it would not have to be a double date.

It meant that when I took a girl out, some other fellow
would not take her up to her door and, for all I knew, get my
good-night kiss. It would be me with my dog who would run

up the front steps, tell my date good night, and come back to the car like a man.

Others who were handicapped could be men again, I thought, as I lay awake, impatient for the morning hours. There must be young men like me all over America who longed to break out of the prison of blindness. Those dogs would liberate us all.

The rising sun found me writing to Dorothy Harrison Eustis, in care of the *Saturday Evening Post*. My father typed as I dictated. "Is what you say really true?" I asked. "If so, I want one of those dogs! And I am not alone. Thousands of blind like me abhor being dependent on others. Help me and I will help them. Train me and I will bring back my dog and show people here how a blind man can be absolutely on his own. We can then set up an instruction center in this country to give all those here who want it a chance at a new life."

My hand trembled as I signed my name to this most significant letter of my life, then tapped my way to the mailbox near our home. I felt for the slot and dropped all my hopes down the narrow opening. The click of the lid signaled a new meaning to my life. It marked the start of a single motivating purpose that was to determine my every action for the next thirty years. At twenty I was a dedicated man.

Then began an agonizing period of waiting for a reply. I started to doubt what Mrs. Eustis had written. I must not let myself be carried away, I told myself. Maybe it was only magazine talk, sensationalism to sell an article. What if there weren't enough dogs to go around? What if the authorities would not let them come into this country? What if the dogs themselves could operate only in familiar German surroundings?

Questions, uncertainties, fears raced through my head. Anguish weighed me down. Was I destined to go on forever, step by timid step, tapping my way through life with a cane?

For thirty agonizing days I went to our mailbox, looking in vain for Mrs. Eustis' answer to my plea.

The next morning I put off my trip to the mailbox, wanting to prolong the possibility of the letter's being there as long as I could. That was the time I should have raced to meet the postman. He had left a letter which I found out bore a bright blue and red Swiss stamp. From her home, "Fortunate Fields," near Vevey in the Swiss Alps had come the reply I had waited for so long. Father read it to me.

Mrs. Eustis explained that she was a Philadelphian, living in Switzerland. She loved dogs, and on her estate, Fortunate Fields, she trained German shepherds for use by the police, the Red Cross, and the Army.

She had never trained any guide dogs for the blind, she went on to say. At this my heart sank. It was a very highly specialized job, she explained. However, she continued, if I really had the courage to come all the way from Tennessee to the mountains of Switzerland in search of a dog, she had a qualified trainer lined up for me.

My heart pounded as Father read on. Mrs. Eustis was coming to Philadelphia for Christmas and would telephone me at that time for my final decision.

Our family was in an uproar. Father was all for my going. He wanted to take me himself, but could not leave his business. Mother had serious misgivings about the long journey. Some friends said, "You're crazy, chasing all the way across the ocean after a dog." Others said, "Morris, it sounds great. What can you lose?"

For an expert opinion I wrote to Dr. Edward E. Allen, a personal friend and director of the Perkins Institute for the Blind. "You have a long life ahead of you," he wrote me. "You have always rebelled against being dependent upon other people. Perhaps this will solve your problem—and not only yours but, if your plan goes through, that of thousands more just like you. You are young, boy. Take a chance, not only for yourself but for others." After this Mother agreed to let me undertake the voyage.

Two weeks later I received a telegram from Mrs. Eustis saying she would telephone that night. Excitement was intense at home as the hour drew near. I took my place by the phone and waited nervously. When it finally rang, I jumped with surprise. Then I heard a quiet, cultivated voice, "Mr. Frank, do you still think you want to come to Switzerland for your dog?"

I could not answer; I was too choked up. That heavenly voice went on, warningly yet encouragingly, "It's a very long trip for a blind boy alone."

"Mrs. Eustis," I fairly shouted, regaining my voice, "to get back my independence, I'd go to hell!"

Chapter 2

I WENT to Switzerland in April as if I were a parcel—by American Express. The experience angered and frustrated me and made me all the more determined to undergo any hardship to overcome dependency on others.

I was put in the charge of a particularly unimaginative steward. Rather than being an attendant, he was more of a jailer in ship's clothing. Each morning I was a prisoner in my locked-from-the-outside cabin until he came to escort me to breakfast. As soon as I finished my coffee, he led me back to my quarters.

At ten he exercised me as if I were a horse, methodically trotting me around the deck. Then he deposited me in a steamer chair. If some friendly passenger invited me to take a stroll, we got only a few feet before my keeper ran up breathless, grasped my elbow, and steered me to my seat again where he could keep an eye on me.

I met a delightful English girl with whom I wanted to be alone in the evening. But we could not escape that sleuthing steward. No matter whether we tried to enjoy the shadows cast by a friendly upper-deck lifeboat or took a remote corner of the ship's lounge, come nine o'clock that pest ferreted us out, took me in tow, and locked me in my cabin for the night. American Express and the captain of that ship certainly took seriously their responsibility to the blind man aboard!

19

"I'll make up for this," I thought grimly, "when they turn me loose in Paris."

Paris! I could hardly wait to get to that city that holds so many treasures of the past and pleasures of the present. I yearned to make my way along the grand boulevards. I wanted to hear the lapping of the Seine against the ancient bridges. The Emperor Napoleon had always been my favorite character of history; I intended to visit his tomb at the Invalides and run my hands over the marble mausoleum in which he lies sleeping.

I looked forward to a stop at a sidewalk café. There I would sip an *apéritif*, listen to the laughter of Métro-bound shopgirls, and overhear the exotic accents of my fellow revelers from all over the world. To me, even the shrill horns of the passing taxicabs were going to be a thrill. Though blind, I meant to savor the delights of the queen of cities.

I got off the boat train at the Gare du Nord and was left alone for what seemed hours and hours.

"Mr. Frank?" finally came the brisk inquiry in a woman's voice with a Parisian accent. It was the representative from American Express.

"You are to come with me, please," she said in a cold, businesslike tone I never thought could belong to a French-woman.

She took me to a little hotel and up to a musty-smelling room.

"A bottle of wine and some biscuits are on the table," she said as she slammed the door behind her.

I felt my way to the bottle and had a glass of wine. Then I groped for the telephone to order some food; I was ravished with hunger. No one spoke English, and I knew no French. I felt my way around the wall to the door—the last ignominy—she had locked it!

In desperation I finished the bottle and crackers and fell asleep. Hours later someone rudely shook me awake.

"Get up, Mr. Frank. It's midnight. Time to go to your train."

It was the woman from American Express. My stay in Europe's loveliest city had come to an end.

I stepped down from my train compartment into the warm sunshine and the fresh cool air of spring in Vevey, Switzerland.

"Mr. Frank, here we are!" were the first welcome words I heard. It was Mrs. Eustis' lovely voice. She shook my hand warmly.

"With me are our director of training and genetics, Jack Humphrey, Mrs. Humphrey, and their little George, who's four," she said, and we shook hands cordially all around.

Mrs. Eustis, this friendly person who had already become such an important part of my life, was small, about five feet two, I judged. By the way she spoke to her chauffeur and the others, she impressed me as being considerate yet firm, one who had high standards of conduct for herself and for others. I could tell she was one who knew how to get what she wanted—a good person to take up one's cause. I sat between her and gentle Mrs. Humphrey on the drive up the narrow, winding roads of Mount Pelerin to the gates of Fortunate Fields.

I was a little bewildered as they described the new world I was entering. The chalet was most impressive, consisting of two spacious connecting buildings, one of three stories, the other rising to four!

We left our hats and coats in a small anteroom, its floor paved by stones worn smooth during generations of use. It opened into a long parlor with a billiard table in the center. At the far end comfortable chairs were set before a fireplace that sent out a cozy warmth and pleasant crackling.

I memorized the layout of my immediate surroundings, using the game room as my starting point. To my left a door opened to Mrs. Eustis' suite. On the right I would have to watch out for the stairway that led up to the dining room. Straight ahead lay a real hazard—a short flight of three steps leading down to a tremendous living room. In one vaulted corner stood a priceless grand piano that belonged to Josef Hoffman, former owner of Fortunate Fields. As I stood beside it, they told me that the room gave on a magnificent view that soared beyond the Swiss border to the mountains of Italy and France. Little George shoved into my hand a picture he had drawn and shyly said, "It's of what you could see, if you could see, out the window!"

After dinner Jack Humphrey told me something about their work. Mrs. Eustis was interested chiefly in breeding a strain of German shepherds with high teachability. To prove them, she trained them for sentry and police duty and rescue work.

Jack was to be my instructor. He had spent a month of highly specialized work in Potsdam to learn the technique. First he had concentrated on the training of guide dogs. That mastered, he studied ways of teaching the blind to use them. I was to be his first pupil. Tomorrow, he said, he would introduce me to my dog, a German shepherd that had been specially selected from the finest of her breed. The day after, we would begin training.

I spent the next morning torn between impatience and nervousness. What would this new animal in my life be like? Would she like me? I knew she was handsome. Mrs. Eustis had described her as a beautiful dark gray with a creamy patch at her throat. Her sensitive ears were always alert, her soft brown eyes brilliant and full of understanding. How I hoped I'd look as good to her as, in my mind's eye, she already did to me.

It was not until afternoon that Jack said, "Morris, I'll bring your dog."

My dog!

"Here's something to give her," he said, putting a small ball of ground meat into my hand. "You must start winning her affection."

He left but in a few minutes returned. I heard the door open and the soft fall of the dog's paws on the floor. I held out the morsel and while she accepted it with dignity, I knelt and patted her, stroking her soft, silky coat.

How lovely she was! And it was in her power to deliver to me the divine gift of freedom! I felt a surge of affection for her.

Jack stood by quietly. "What's her name?" I asked him.

"Kiss," he answered.

"Kiss!" I exclaimed. My face turned red as I pictured my embarrassment at calling out, "Here, Kiss! Come, Kiss!" in a crowd of strangers. "That's a hell of a name for a dog," I told him brusquely. Then I put my arms around my new friend and told her, "I'm going to call you Buddy."

I took Buddy's leash and made a fuss over her all afternoon. Already attached to her trainers and fond of her playmates in the kennel, she merely tolerated me. She was pleased that night, however, to be taken to sleep beside my bed in my warm room, instead of to the dogs' quarters.

Cold air racing off the snow-capped mountains next morning caused me to snuggle down under the blankets and resist coming to consciousness. Then a warm tongue licked my face. I remembered I was in Switzerland, on top of Mount Pelerin, and this was Buddy. All that had happened to me in the past few weeks had not been a dream.

I got up, dressed, and took Buddy down the outside stairs to the yard to take care of her morning needs. We then proceeded to the dining room, where the family had gathered at the breakfast table by the bay window overlooking Lake Léman. After delicious wild strawberries with rich Alpine cream and strong black coffee Jack pushed his chair back and said, "Well, it's time to go to work, Morris."

At last my training was to begin. I went back to my room, buckled on Buddy's harness, and met Jack at the front door.

"Pick up your handle in your left hand—the dog always works on your left side, between you and pedestrian traffic," Jack said in a quiet, firm voice. "Keep your shoulders back and walk with the stride of a soldier.

"Now give the command 'Forward' and give it clearly. As soon as the dog responds, reward her with praise."

I took the harness, my heart pounding, and said, somewhat shakily, "Forward!" Then, "That's a good girl!" The handle almost jerked out of my hand, and we simply flew to the gate. Buddy stopped before it, and for a moment I teetered back and forth and almost lost my balance.

"She's showing you where the latch is," said Jack.

I put my hand on her head, slid it down her nose, and found she could not have indicated the location of the latch more accurately if she had been a teacher with a wooden pointer. I lifted it and we started through.

"Keep your free arm close to your side or you'll hit the gate post," warned Jack.

Following Jack's instructions, I gave the commands "Right" and "Forward"—this time a little less timidly—and down the road we went at a clip I had not gone in years. I heard, "Keep your shoulders back." As I straightened, I unconsciously threw out my chest. My stride lengthened and I heard Mrs. Eustis' voice saying, "Look, his head has gone up!"

No wonder! It was glorious—just a dog and a leather strap linking me to life. We were bound for Vevey—a funicular ride away and down the mountain side from Fortunate Fields. I was keenly aware of the people, the dog carts, the push carts, the horses and wagons on the sloping road leading to the small depot. As I was visualizing the jostle and enjoying the crisp air, Buddy abruptly stopped. "Ah, the funicular steps, probably," I thought, and slid my foot forward. Sure enough, there was a low platform! How exciting! "Forward! That's a good girl!" I cried. I felt Buddy's harness tilt, giving me a gentle pull, and up we went.

Jack sat with us when we found places on the cable car.

"Put the dog under your knees so no one steps on her," he said. I felt the jerking start of the tension-controlled car, and twenty minutes later we had grated our way down the hill to the center of the little city.

My first blurred memory of Vevey is a mélange of commands and swift, exhilarating walk, of the sound of the clopping of horses' hoofs on stone streets and the chatter of people whose language I could not understand. Then more stops, more commands, and more curbs.

On a narrow sidewalk the feel of the harness told me Buddy was swerving to the right, and I swerved with her. "She just took you around a man carrying two big bushel baskets of beans," said Jack.

Buddy stopped. I pushed my foot forward but felt nothing. Jack laughed. "It's not a step," he explained. "A woman stopped in front of you. Give Buddy the 'Forward' command."

I did, and we skirted the obstacle. "That mother was blocking the way with a baby carriage and Buddy had to wait for her to move her youngster before we could get by," Jack said.

At one point Buddy deftly swung out to the left, then back in line again. I felt no presence of person or building nearby. "Why did she do that?" I asked Jack.

"Put your hand up," was his reply.

I did, and at about eye level hit an iron pipe, the framework support of an awning. It would have struck me right in the face but for Buddy. This, to me, seemed the most amazing guiding she had done. Traveling alone, she would hardly have noticed that heavy structure, so far above her, but with me in tow, her eyes had measured it against my six feet. She had received no command, she acted entirely on her own responsibility. When she did that, she was thinking! Hers were, indeed, my seeing eyes. *"That's a good girl!"* I said with feeling.

Each new experience gave me more the feel of the harness, the ability to relax, and increased my trust in Buddy. For two hours Jack constantly interpreted the movements of my dog and reminded me to walk erectly and not grip the lead-rein too tightly. Buddy worked with a gay air, tail wagging, as though she enjoyed knowing so much more than I did.

It was so exciting that not until I reached home and sank into a comfortable chair did I realize how exhausted I was. My feet hurt, the muscles of my legs ached from the unaccustomed exercise, my left arm was sore and my back hurt from pulling against the harness. But these aches added up to the best feeling I had had in years.

After we had taken a morning and an afternoon excursion each day for five days, Jack said, "Tomorrow, you're on your own. I'll follow at some distance behind you, but I won't interfere."

I trembled inwardly. With every trip Jack had become more strict. He did not tolerate mind-wandering. If I was carried away by the exhilaration of a brisk walk, he would bring me back to earth with a gruff prompting that I was in training. He was an excellent coach.

"You'll get no more reminders," he warned. "If you don't do what I've tried to teach you, you may get a good bump. That'll penetrate that thick skull of yours!"

I listened, thinking hopefully, "He wouldn't dare let me get hurt."

When Buddy and I appeared at the front door next morn-

ing, Jack carefully reviewed for me every turn and block of
the route to the city and back. Then, for the first time, we set
out on our own.

At the gate, instead of stopping immediately when Buddy
did, I took two steps and ran smack into the post. There was
Jack's big laugh behind me and a hearty, "I told you, but you
wouldn't listen."

I lifted the latch, pretending I had done nothing more than
brush the gate post, and laughed back.

"Forward and right," I commanded. Buddy did not move.
Jack said not a word. "Oh, I mean—right, forward!" I corrected myself, disconcerted to have made two errors in about
two minutes. I felt Buddy's tail wag, and on our way we went.

Buddy paused as usual at the steps to the funicular, but I
was nervous and did not halt myself promptly. I stumbled and
fell down, giving my knees a good thwacking. Jack did not
even say, "Did you hurt yourself?" He just laughed. Brushing
off the dust, I clenched my teeth and thought, "That's a mean
way to treat a blind man."

I took a seat in the cable car and, immersed in my own
chagrin, allowed Buddy to flop down in front of me without
seeing to it that her feet were well out of people's way. Jack
purposely stepped on her paw and she yelped. I hastily put
her under my knees as I was supposed to do and sat there, a
very dejected fellow. That cable car did not plummet any
faster downhill than did my own spirits.

Jack did not speak to us. "Why does he laugh at me like
that?" I thought, resentfully. "Why didn't he save me from
falling? And why did he feel it was necessary to step on my
dog just to teach me a lesson?"

In Vevey, feeling discouraged and still angry at Jack, I followed Buddy lackadaisically, although she was moving with
alacrity. My shoulder grazed several people, a forceful and
humiliating reminder to bring my arm in closer to my side.

By the time we reached our first corner, I was in a boiling rage and did not listen for the sound of traffic, as Jack had instructed. Rashly I gave my command, "Forward." Halfway across, Buddy made an abrupt stop, then hurriedly backed up, dragging me with her. I felt a car zoom past, so close that its rear wheels threw stinging gravel in my face. That brought me to my senses. When we reached the safety of the opposite curb, I gave her a big, heartfelt hug.

On the return trip to Fortunate Fields I did better. I relaxed more and followed my guide with an easier gait. But I had not relaxed my attitude toward Jack.

"I don't want any lunch," I said when we got back to the house, and went right on up to my room.

I was lying on the bed telling Buddy how unfairly I was being treated when I heard the door open and someone enter.

"Look, boy"—it was Jack's voice. "You have your choice: you can be just another blind man or you can be a man on your own with Buddy's eyes to help you. You can't lean on me. If I have to follow you and tell you everything, you aren't going to depend on your dog. You won't be able to master the signals."

I didn't answer.

"When you go back to the United States," Jack continued, "I won't be there. Your future's up to you."

He had quietly closed the door before I realized he was gone. I was ashamed. Jack wasn't unsympathetic, I told myself. He was absolutely right.

That night I went to bed feeling lonely and discouraged. What if I couldn't learn to use a guide dog, after all? What if my concentration was too poor? What if I couldn't communicate with Buddy? What a fool I'd feel returning to Nashville and admitting I'd been a failure. Other blind I wanted to help would never even know I'd tried.

It came over me with a rush that I was a far piece from

home; an ocean and a foreign country separated me from those who loved me. For the first time I felt really homesick.

Then, as if she knew how low-spirited I was, Buddy got up from her place by my bed. She crawled up on top of the covers beside me, nuzzled the back of my neck, and snuggled as close to me as she could, giving a long low grunt of contentment and companionship.

Her warm affection completely changed my mental attitude. In reviewing the morning, I thought it had not been so bad, really. I had made mistakes, but I had learned a lot from them. I had done fairly well on the last part of the trip. Even Jack had said that was so. "A pretty good job," he'd told me, "for your first run without help."

Most important, Buddy had shown me that if I did my part, we two would walk together in safety. My heartache gone, I dropped off to sleep with the comfort of Buddy close beside me.

That night a partnership was born, the beginning of a life together—a man and a dog, a man whose dog meant to him emancipation, a new world, and other worlds to conquer.

Our training trips became more difficult. Jack mapped out trial runs for Buddy and me that forced us to learn to move together under all conditions. One day we had an unexpected test of our responses. As we trudged up the narrow way from the cable car, my ears were assailed by a heavy rumble and a wild clatter of staccato hoofbeats.

"Runaway horses!" I thought as the turmoil bore down upon us. I was helpless to know which way to turn to escape. But not Buddy! She lunged to the right, off the side of the road, with such force she almost jerked me off my feet. Then the harness handle tilted until I was reaching up over my head to maintain my grasp, and she had me stumbling up a steep embankment. She literally hauled me up the seven-foot rocky slope. We stopped, panting, at the top—out of the way just in time as the team of snorting, mad animals careened past, dragging a hurtling, crashing wagon.

When it was all over and I had come down and patted and praised Buddy, I suddenly realized that Jack had seen the whole episode. Too far behind to help, he had simply held his breath and prayed that we would survive the emergency. Thanks to Buddy, we did.

As the lessons progressed, my powers of concentration increased so that when listening to directions I never had to ask that they be repeated. I gave my commands in a loud, clear voice, aimed straight at the back of Buddy's head; my vocal chords grew stronger. I became more sensitive to Buddy's communications. I could even tell if she moved her head to the left or right.

Jack now trusted us to find our way about Vevey without his following close behind. After accompanying us down the hill in the cable car, he would then send us off on our own. We became a familiar duo on the little city's cobblestone streets, and received many greetings. By now I could recognize and reply to the individual *"Bon jours!"* of the postman, the flower lady, and the underworked *gendarme*.

Buddy and I sped swiftly about on the itineraries Jack laid out for us. He and I customarily had a glass of beer at the depot's sidewalk café if I got back before the cable car arrived. It didn't take long until I was making Jack's mapped-out tours in time to have two beers before the car came. This, I thought, was worthwhile progress.

I typed happy letters to my mother and father: "Think of it—being able to go where I please. You know I haven't wept in four years, but when that dog pilots me safely across the street with automobiles whizzing past all around us, I just feel like sitting down on the pavement, throwing my arms around her neck, and crying." When I thought that all the blind in America might have this same kind of protective companionship, my exhilaration was multiplied a thousandfold.

But it was not all beer and skittles. One day I stopped at a Vevey crossing with Buddy and felt an authoritative tug at my coat sleeve. A lady with a clipped British accent then told me, "Young man, it's an outrageous thing to put a poor dog into slavery!"

"Ma'am," I said, patiently, "this dog knows she is loved, belongs, and is needed. She's not turned out in the morning when children go to school and left to fend for herself until they get back in the afternoon. Nobody throws rocks at her, and her water pan is not left dirty or empty. When this dog is hungry, she doesn't have to turn over a garbage pail."

A disapproving silence told me it would take *some* talking to convince this woman.

"What a dog wants more than anything else is human companionship," I went on. "In return for the love and affection I give her and for keeping her well groomed and clean and cared for, she gladly serves as my eyes."

My lecture not only failed to persuade her; it made her irate.

"My good fellow," she said, and I pictured her clenching her teeth and shaking an umbrella, "if you came all this way from the United States, you must have money. Why don't you hire somebody there to take care of you and lead you about? Why do you have to come over here and enslave a poor foreign dog?"

And, to clinch her argument, she demanded, bitingly, "Aren't you a Christian?"

With that, I tipped my hat and said, "No, Ma'am, I am a Mohammedan! Buddy, forward!"

One other encounter with an Englishwoman left me feeling rather sorry for the lady.

"When will your dog have puppies?" she asked.

I explained that Buddy was a career girl, destined never to become a mother.

"Oh, dear, the poor thing," she murmured sympathetically. "She'll always be an old maid, just like me!"

I had been at Fortunate Fields several weeks when one morning I said to Mrs. Eustis, "I'd like to get a haircut. I guess I'll ask Jack to take me to the barber shop."

"Take yourself," she answered. "You have your dog."

What a challenge! I had never made the round trip to the city—portal to portal—alone all the way. My hands became moist and I felt warm all over with excitement. It would be the first time I dared set out on my own initiative, without leaning on Jack.

"Forward, Buddy!" my voice rang out.

My senses seemed sharpened as she and I followed the familiar pattern of paths that led from gate to funicular and to Vevey itself.

Now I repeated over and over to myself the directions I had been given. I felt like a child trying to find his way through a maze—only this wasn't a game, this was in earnest. What if I got hopelessly lost? What if I failed to find the barber and had to return home, not only shaggy thatched but a failure as well?

I counted the curbs as we passed by the village shops. The clucking of hens told me I had arrived at the poultryman's corner. I turned left. Soon I smelled the fragrance from the crusty loaves at the bakery and I was reassured that we were on the right track.

"Right, Buddy," I said.

Then, suddenly, borne on the heavenly scent of bay rum, I heard the barber's cheery "Good morning, Monsieur!"

I'm sure that man never had a more enthusiastic, happy response to any greeting he had ever tendered in his long career of scissors-wielding!

My haircut pleased me as much as if it had been specially designed and executed for me by the famous hairdresser at the Ritz, and my pal Buddy and I made the trip home as if on wings, rather than propelled by our combined six feet.

I sat down in the living room, threw back my head and laughed, roared until the tears came to my eyes.

"What's got into you, Morris?" asked Mrs. Eustis.

"Ma'am," I said, "I've been blind since I was sixteen. For years someone has had to take me to the barber shop. I've been left waiting there like unclaimed luggage for hours at a time. Sometimes my father would deposit me on his way to work at nine and I would have to sit there until he came back to pick me up at noon. Today when I mentioned a haircut to you, you told me where to go for it and how to get there. I took my dog, or rather, my dog took me, I got my own haircut and came back. Now for the first time I'm convinced that I am really going to be free. That's why I'm laughing—because I'm free, by God, I'm free!"

No sighted person could ever understand the magnitude of my relief. I felt like a bound eagle that had been loosed to soar again. I had maintained a smile on my face since I was a teen-ager, to keep up a front. This was my first genuine laugh in four years.

As the time drew near for me to "graduate" and go back home, Mrs. Eustis, Jack, and I had long conferences about my plans for an organization to bring Buddies to the blind in America. Where would we begin? Who would provide the money? Could we find a sufficient number of intelligent dogs in the U.S.? Who there could train them and teach the blind to use them?

We thought it might be best to plan to begin with an office in Nashville, since that was my home and it was also fairly centrally located. We could branch out from there. It would

be ideal if we could get help from already established charitable agencies for the blind. Many strategically situated
throughout the various regions of the country already had
housing accommodations, grounds—and money to spend on
rehabilitation. If they would join us with such facilities and
financial aid, we could start almost immediately. We could
begin right away to train as many of the blind as available
dogs and instructors would permit. Failing agency cooperation,
depending on our own limited funds, we would have to start
on a very modest scale indeed.

Fortunate Fields could supply a few dogs and trainers in the
beginning. If things went well, the entire staff and kennels
could, if necessary, be converted to helping supply the needs
of the new enterprise.

"All this is looking far ahead," said Mrs. Eustis. "Whether
any school for guide dogs can ever get started at all depends
upon two things very close at hand. Number one, although
we here are confident that Buddy can give you complete freedom of movement, few people at home will believe it. And
even we cannot say for certain how a dog trained here in little
Vevey will perform in the unfamiliar, perhaps confusing,
conditions of U.S. metropolitan areas. You and Buddy will
have to go from city to city and prove beyond the shadow of
a doubt that it is not only possible for you to get about but
that it is practically as easy for you as for any sighted person."

That was, indeed, a large order. I shuddered as I visualized
the traffic bedlam of Chicago's "Loop."

"Number two," Mrs. Eustis continued, "you must not
forget that signs saying 'No Dogs Allowed' are almost everywhere—in restaurants, hotels, office buildings, and stores. If
the blind man's dog can't be with him in the places he has
to go, of what value is it to him? And what about restrictions
on trains, streetcars, and busses? If a person can't use his dog
to get to work, it's obvious he can't hold down a job. How

will it ever be possible for the organization to succeed unless the guide dogs are welcome in all public places?"

It was a sobering thought.

"So, your second task," she concluded, "is to get Buddy accepted all over America with no more fuss than if she were a cane."

This would be far from easy. It would take phenomenal effort before Buddy would be permitted even to stick her cold nose into many establishments I could think of. Once she was in them, only a very convincing demonstration of good conduct could persuade those in charge to relax rules of many years' standing.

"On my last trip to the States," Mrs Eustis went on, "I remember seeing some blind beggars on the streets with dogs as companions. The thought of those defeated-looking tin cups still makes me cringe. You, Morris, must set a new picture in the public mind. You must hold your head high and make a blind man and his dog now stand for dignity and self-reliance."

Doubts assailed me. Was I taking on an assignment that I would never be able to carry out?

"Of course this last part of your groundwork will require some long spadings," said Mrs. Eustis, as if reading my thoughts. "It takes time to break down prejudice. But you can judge Buddy's prowess in strange traffic by the time you get back to Nashville. Stop over in every large city on the way and put her to the acid test in every one of them. Don't spare her. If you and she meet the challenge and prove that the blind and their dogs can successfully negotiate the traffic of America's city streets, I will guarantee ten thousand dollars and send a staff to help you start the guide dog school."

We talked about a name for my proposed organization.

"I'd like to call it 'The Seeing Eye,'" I told Mrs. Eustis, "The title of the article that brought us together."

"I think that would be very appropriate, Morris," she answered. "It's from a Book that has been an unsurpassed guide itself for centuries: Proverbs 20:12, 'The hearing ear, and the seeing eye, the Lord hath made even both of them.'"

When it was time for *"au revoir,"* Mrs. Eustis, Jack, Mrs. Humphrey, and little George drove Buddy and me to the station, and they wished us Godspeed.

"Morris, you're a far cry from the timid, stooped, uncertain boy we met here less than six weeks ago," said Mrs. Eustis as she pressed my hand in farewell. "We're *so* proud of you!"

I had no words with which to thank her. My heart was too full. I would always be grateful to all of them. They would never know—I myself could hardly tell—what the days had done for me. Fortunate Fields were aptly named, I thought. They had restored my self-confidence.

I pulled my shoulders back, I took a deep breath, threw out my chest, and stood as tall as I could. I felt ready for the tremendous job ahead: to try to make it possible for my fellow American blind to sign their Declaration of Independence.

Chapter 3

~~~~~~~~~~

*T*HE coming back, the coming home, the being free! Paris was Paris to me this time. I had two days there and I worked out a good system. I would simply take an American dollar bill and wave it until I found a cab driver who could speak English. That way Buddy and I missed few of the high spots. We rode up the "sideways" elevator to the top of the Eiffel Tower, we strolled in the Tuileries and listened to the splashing fountains and the shouts of little boys sailing their boats in the turbulent basins. The exhilarating pop of champagne corks punctuated our trips to the sidewalk cafés and night clubs. We took part in as much of the joyous life of that gay city as we could reach. Buddy never told during her lifetime all the things we did in those two wonderful days, and now I am not going to tell either. You can just imagine what a twenty-year-old boy, foot-loose and on his own, would do in Paris.

Above and beyond my memories of Paris as a city of pleasure is that of her as a place of inspiration and dedication. I shall never forget our pilgrimage to the tomb of Napoleon. It was after visiting hours when we arrived, but the guard, a very decent fellow, exercised his French right to make decisions in individual cases and personally escorted me down to the revered vaulted room I so wanted to visit. I could literally feel the great emperor's presence. Buddy, too, seemed strangely affected. I placed one hand on the cold marble and the other on her faithful head. "You, too, Buddy, will lead an army," I said to myself. "It won't be like Napoleon's, but an army of men and women fighting, praying for their independence. You will be the general, first of all the leaders of the free blind." I believed it was Buddy's destiny to do more for humanity than any other dog in history.

How different was the trip back on the boat!

I was not just a blind boy herded hither and yon by impatient attendants. I was a free man who knew what he wanted and was capable of getting it. The steward demonstrated the layout of our cabin, the smoking room, bar, reception room, deck, bath, and all around the ship. That was all we needed; I knew where I wanted to go. All I had to do was give Buddy the commands.

We were topside bright and early the first morning out for a brisk turn around the deck before breakfast. We went to dine any time during lunch and dinner hours that we felt like it, not when a steward felt like taking us. We strolled the steamer as we pleased, and no one grabbed my arm and set me in a chair when I wanted to be somewhere else. At night they dared not lock us in our cabin at nine; some nights we hardly got to bed at all.

Buddy's brilliance, affectionate nature, and responsiveness won everyone's heart. Through her I made more friends the first hour on deck than during the entire trip to Europe. We had great fun. We won money at deck horse racing and enjoyed the concerts and dance music. We were even on the captain's deck; Buddy was the first dog, the captain said, ever to be there. She seemed to enjoy it like an old seadog and stood there looking far out to sea.

As we neared the end of the voyage, I went to the purser's office to have my passport verified and to exchange my French money for U.S. currency. Leaving, I put my wallet inside my coat pocket and started back to my cabin, a journey that took us through the entire ship. We twisted and turned through a labyrinth of passages, up and down companionways, all the way from first to tourist class. That's quite a tour even for a sighted person.

As I lay down on my bunk to nap, Buddy touched me on the arm with her paw, but I paid no attention. Again I felt her, but ignored her. Then she put her forefeet up on me and dropped something on my chest. When I reached for it, I discovered that it was my wallet. Evidently it had missed my pocket and fallen on the deck. She had picked it up and carried it while guiding me all the way.

Besides being grateful to her for saving me from a serious loss, I was deeply touched that she had acted entirely on her own initiative. It suggested to me that Buddy apparently knew that I was blind. She certainly realized that I belonged to her, was her responsibility. Just as she sometimes actually disobeyed an order from me if following it would bring me harm, she was on the lookout to protect me without any orders at all.

Our first real challenge came when one of a crowd of reporters who met the boat in New York dared me to cross West Street. I had never heard of West Street. If I had, I would not have answered so confidently. Much wider than Fifth Avenue, it runs along the Hudson River waterfront and carries the heaviest kind of traffic. But it was just another street to me. "Brother," I said, "you show us where it is and we'll cross it."

It's right here," he said.

"Okay," I replied. "Buddy, forward."

We entered a street so noisy it was almost like entering a wall of sound.

She went about four paces and halted. A deafening roar

and a rush of hot air told me a tremendous truck was swooshing past so near that Buddy could have lifted her nose and touched it.

She moved forward again into the ear-splitting clangor, stopped, backed up, and started again. I lost all sense of direction and surrendered myself entirely to the dog. I shall never forget the next three minutes. Ten-ton trucks rocketing past, cabs blowing their horns in our ears, drivers shouting at us. One fellow yelled, "You damned fool, do you want to get killed?"

When we finally got to the other side and I realized what a really magnificent job she had done, I leaned over and gave Buddy a great big hug and told her what a good, good girl she was.

"She sure is a good girl," exclaimed a voice at my elbow— one of the photographers. "I had to come over in a cab, and some of the fellows who tried to cross with you are still back on the other side!"

Forty-second Street at Fifth Avenue was next. Though everybody thought that our performance was spectacular, it was easy compared to the pandemonium of West Street. It was so jammed with people that about all Buddy had to do was follow the crowd. Trailed everywhere by photographers and newsmen helping break the story to the U.S., we went to every tough intersection reporters or friends could suggest. It was most exciting. At night, linked by a light grasp on Buddy's harness handle, we negotiated Broadway's Great White Way from Forty-second to Fiftieth streets, continually crossing and recrossing from one side to the other.

I could tell from the signals I received through the handle that the flashing neon signs and the loud clang that accompanied the changing of the traffic lights from red to green bothered her somewhat. She would turn her head alertly from side to side, but neither lights nor noise nor the obstacles of sidewalk roasting stands of hot-chestnut vendors could stay us from our appointed rounds.

Everywhere, of course, people were attracted to Buddy. They spoke to her, petted her, offered her sweets. But she refused to be distracted, did not get irritated or sidetracked, and did her work magnificently and with obvious pleasure. In a week Buddy had conquered the biggest city in the world. She was a celebrity, in a town that loves nothing better.

I am thankful to the newspaper people who chronicled her every move. We were accomplishing the first part of my self-appointed task—to let the world know that a Seeing Eye dog could really be a pair of eyes.

Before leaving New York, I visited an important agency for the blind. The director, a blind man himself, listened politely while I unfolded to him my plan. I would work six months or a year, proving the value of the guide dog, then return to my insurance business. An agency such as his should then take over the organization we had started and expand it.

"Mr. Frank," he said coldly, "I personally feel that it's bad enough to be blind without being tied to a dog."

This was the first of a series of disillusioning interviews, there and later in other cities, with professional workers with the blind. Many did excellent work, but others simply represented the kind of blind who could or would not accept the challenge of getting out and doing for themselves.

While no one enjoys blindness, numbers of people, blind and sighted, in all income groups, enjoy being helpless and letting someone else take care of them. Our work would appeal to that very special breed of men and women who would put up a real fight to regain self-reliance. I gave up hope of help from the charitable agencies. We were going to have to start from scratch.

We did not come up against the "No Dogs Allowed" half of my assignment in New York. While there, I stayed with my friend Nathan at a small hotel on Seventy-fifth Street where the management treated Buddy as the personification of "man's best friend." It was a different question, though, when, our work completed in New York, we set out for Philadelphia on the first lap of our journey home to Nashville.

When I started to board the train, the conductor put a restraining hand on my arm and said, "You can't bring that dog on the train."

"You're right," I told him. "The dog is going to bring *me* on. Buddy, forward!"

Buddy went right in, found me a seat, and curled up under it. Angrily the conductor followed us and reached down to take her away. Buddy just looked at him and showed her beautiful white teeth. He hesitated, then punched my ticket, returned it with vehemence, and that was the end of "The Case of the Frustrated Conductor." It seemed to me just another proof that Buddy could handle any situation intelligently—with or without orders from me!

In Philadelphia Buddy found no barriers, as we had the fortunate backing not only of Mrs. Eustis' family, the Harrisons, but also of wonderful old Mr. Asa Wing, president of the Provident Mutual Insurance Company, for which I worked, then as now. Buddy completely captivated him. We walked right into the big dining room for V.I.P.'s only, Buddy trotting proudly with us—a perfect lady accompanied by her two admirers.

Sponsored by Provident Mutual, we found a warm welcome at the Benjamin Franklin Hotel. Buddy took me without interference into the dining salon, the lobby, and the writing rooms.

For the press, to further our educational campaign, Buddy demonstrated her prowess. She took me safely around or over, as the obstacle required, lamp posts, letter boxes, trees growing out of sidewalks, and gutters running with very wet rain water. Countless photographs were taken at Independence Square, where unpredictable performers on roller skates, scooters, and express wagons were as skillfully avoided as if Buddy were an All-American running top-caliber interference on a football field.

She was a great hit. By the time we were ready to leave Philadelphia, Buddy carried with her a great portion of that city's famous Brotherly Love.

When we hit the Sinton Hotel in Cincinnati, we had the advantage that my family was known there. In fact, the only halt to our progress in that city came from a lovely, elderly aunt of my mother's. As we went up her front steps, she called out, "Just leave the dog outside, Morris dear, and come on in."

Her attitude brought home to me the magnitude of the job I had taken on. We had merely scratched the surface when it came to getting guide dogs accepted at their true worth. Leave my eyes on the porch, indeed! I told Aunty, "No Buddy, no Morris," and we three then had a cozy visit.

Leaving Cincinnati, they forced me, despite all my protests, to put Buddy in the baggage car. In the middle of the night the conductor shook me awake in my lower berth and said, "The dog is loose. Please come and tie her up again."

I put on bathrobe and slippers and set off down the narrow aisles very unsteadily. Buddy greeted me with great glee, as if we'd been parted for days, and while I was hugging her, the conductor departed. When I tied Buddy again and started to leave, I found that the scoundrel had neatly locked me in!

Feeling around for a place to sit, I came upon a long, comfortable box against one wall, stretched out on it and Buddy nudged her way up beside me. When the train stopped at Louisville and people entered the baggage car, I learned to my horror that we were sleeping on top of someone's coffin!

That frightened me so badly that while we were in the station I got off the train with Buddy, walked outside on the platform until I found my Pullman, and climbed on, the conductor fussing all the time. Ignoring him, I told Buddy to jump into the lower and I crawled in after her, leaving the train officials to think what they pleased—no more coffins for me!

This experience inspired a new technique for railroad travel. For the rest of our journey I made it a point to make a reservation, invariably a lower, on a night train. We would catch it just before it pulled out. The conductor thought he would just permit the dog to show me the berth, then he would hustle her back to the baggage car. But Buddy immediately parted the curtains and hopped in the bed.

Though she was a very sweet-tempered girl, she was a dog you could not fool with. If the conductor seized her leash and tried to take her away from me, she braced herself, looked him straight in the eye, growled ominously, and that was that.

On the final lap of our journey we found a delightful surprise in the new daytime conductor. He scolded me in a very loud voice. "No dogs allowed!" he said. "It's against regulations. I'll have to call the police!" Then he leaned over and whispered in my ear, so the other passengers could not hear, "Put your legs back against the seat so the dog cannot get her feet in the aisle and be stepped on." Then he headed in the direction of the dining car. He had done his duty and a good deed.

Then home! Home to my friends and home to Nashville as a conquering hero, though actually Buddy was the real heroine. She had led her blind charge successfully on a voyage over the Atlantic and halfway across the American continent.

We had traveled thousands of miles, using all kinds and means of transportation. We had stayed in new and strange places. We had met hundreds of people and made hundreds of friends. We had deliberately sought out dangerous intersections, narrow, curbless streets, fast and congested traffic to prove our *rapport*. Never had the principles mastered and tested under conditions abroad failed us when applied here. Buddy had clearly demonstrated that well-educated dogs could guide the blind safely through the biggest and most complicated cities the world could offer. She was indeed my "seeing eye."

As we stepped into the car where my blind mother was waiting, Buddy licked her arm and her hand as much as to say, "I bring you, ma'am, a new son, a seeing child again."

When I kissed my mother, her face was wet, and I thought she understood what Buddy was telling her.

My father—oh, how he loved that dog from the first moment! She could do no wrong. My greatest problem with him was to be to keep him from spoiling her.

Buddy looked over all the family as they came in to meet her. She gave a wag of her bushy tail to some, to others a kiss, jumping up and licking them on the face. Those less favored received a polite snubbing. Remarkably, she must have caught a cue from some subtle tone of my voice as I introduced each, for she showed affection for those I liked and was less cordial to those of whom I was not quite so fond.

It was good to be home.

Next morning early Buddy and I hopped a streetcar with a friendly motorman. We were bound for Western Union.

"I want to send a cable. Address it, 'Eustis, Mount Pelerin, Switzerland,'" I told the clerk.

"Yes, sir. What is the message?"

"success."

"Is that all?" he asked incredulously. "Just one word?"

"Brother," I told him, "that tells everything."

Chapter 4

O F COURSE we had only started. In Nashville, for example, we had to get all the streetcars open to Buddy —her job was not only to take me to college and to work; she had to blaze the trail for other dogs I hoped would follow after her.

It was a difficult job. Some motormen simply ignored the company rule and let us ride. But when I went up to catch a car, I never knew whether I would be allowed to take my dog on or not. Finally I had quite a long interview with a judge representing the company. I think he was more blind than I was. "Son," he asked, at the end of an hour's talk, "is this the best way you know to get yourself killed?"

I could see that it was going to be a lot of work to get that blasted first word taken off the streetcar placards that read "No Dogs Allowed."

My insurance office was in the First and Fourth National Bank Building. The bank's attorney was quite concerned about having a dog riding up and down on the elevators, and he spoke to the president, Mr. James Caldwell, about it.

"Mr. Jimmie" called in the attorney and me. "Percy," he said to the lawyer, "you have three children. You don't know what will happen to them as life goes on. Some of them may become incapacitated. This boy, once helpless, has found a

46

way to come and go as he needs to, without being dependent on others. You and I have no right to stand in his way."

The attorney started to protest, and Mr. Jimmie's temper flared. "I don't give a damn what the law says. For God's sake, man, put not obstacles in the way of people handling their problems with dignity!"

We had no further trouble at the First and Fourth.

Life was so much freer for me now in Nashville. My previous four years had been terribly thwarting. I had tried for twelve months to get around with a cane. Once I went into a freshly dug ditch over my head and spent a miserable hour there. You can imagine my humiliation at having to be hauled out of the dirty hole.

Another, more serious time a driver crashed into a curb to keep from hitting me. His car turned completely over. Fortunately no one was hurt. These were only two of many nerve-racking experiences that showed me a cane was not much good to me.

I then hired a boy to guide me for ten dollars a week. Many mornings he did not show up, and I had to miss classes at Vanderbilt. This was tough on my educational progress; I couldn't get much from lectures I didn't even hear. Often when I came out of my classrooms, he would be asleep in the basement and I could not find him nor my next class.

After school hours, when he took me to sell insurance, sometimes people who did not want to be bothered would signal to him that they were "not in," and he would fall in with their subterfuge.

Despite his incompetence and disloyalty, one day while he was guiding me, he insisted on a raise in wages. When I told him I could not agree until he mended his ways, he quit right then and there, leaving me stranded in the middle of busy Broad Street.

Those former days that began with little hope, progressed

to full-fledged frustration, and so often ended in despair were over. Now Buddy took me wherever I wanted to go, whenever I liked. I revisited playgrounds of my childhood that I had not been to for years. We renewed my youth by a trip out into the country by the old rock at the swimming hole. I had yearned to go there again, and I could not have had a happier companion.

Buddy loved her work. She loved her harness. I had merely to hold it out to her and she would bound to me and wriggle into it all by herself. Many were the soul-restoring hours we spent together in familiar, narrow lanes, whose old trees I visualized clearly from my memories. I felt that I was seeing again the colors of those leaves of autumn floating gently down and settling in our path.

Buddy was at home in the city equally as well as in the country. We walked through downtown streets at a free-swinging pace that amazed the general public of Nashville. "B.B."—before Buddy—few outside my immediate circle knew me. If I wandered off the sidewalk a few blocks from my home, people would not refer to me by name, but would call out from their windows to a passerby, "Put the blind boy back on the walk."

Now I heard them say, "Oh, look, there comes Morris and his dog."

"Morris!" Once again, I was a person in my own right. Once again I had a name, like a normal human being. I was glad not to be "that blind boy."

Now strangers spoke freely to me. In the old days, at a street-car stop, for instance, I often envied two sighted persons, who obviously did not know each other, their ease in striking up a conversation. One would remark on the weather or something just as ordinary and start the ball rolling. I think they might have wanted to include me, but they did not know how to get my attention. They did not wish to be rude, leaving me out, but they just did not know how to go about bringing me in without referring to my blindness. With Buddy there, however, it was the easiest and most natural thing in the world for them to say, "What a lovely dog you have!" I'd tell them her name and how smart she was, and the talk went on just as fast as Buddy's tail and my tongue could wag.

I was lucky. In addition to the new friends I was making, I had loyal old friends in Nashville. About six of us fellows did everything together. It was wonderful for me, because, besides having their masculine companionship, we all double-dated, or dozen-dated, so I met many more girls than I otherwise would have.

I remember the first country-club dance. I had received the mailed notice of the party, but was too shy to make plans to go. The boys came by and found me in slacks and sport shirt.

"Aren't you ready?" Al asked.

"No, I'm not going."

"That's not what we asked. Are you coming like you are, or do you intend to go upstairs and dress properly?"

After this there were no more questions; I did everything the rest of the crowd did. In fact, in compensating for not being able to see, I tried to outdo the others. One night at a dance I told someone what I thought about him in no uncertain language. He said that if I weren't blind he would poke me in the nose. Perry walked up and said, "*I'm* not blind," and had it out with him. Then the boys took me aside and gave me a pummeling for getting them into a fight.

This kind of day-to-day life, my major contacts not with psychiatrists or professional workers with the handicapped, but with a group that was normal and treated me as if I were, helped me more than I can say.

Buddy became a part of the gang. Everyone loved her. Thanks to her, I was no longer the thwarted individual who had to be looked out for. I could join the excursions "on the town" instead of restricting most of our group get-togethers to our house. We played rough with Buddy, pushing her around, letting her bark, jump, and do all kinds of things no Seeing Eye dog was supposed to do. But she was my key to emancipation, and we spoiled her.

When the boys came to the house, Buddy was pleased as a puppy and would bound for them, planting her forepaws on their chests in greeting. Some liked this boisterous reception, but for others it was too much. After all, sixty-nine pounds of effusiveness could almost knock you down. Many is the time Buddy has worn out her welcome with one joyous leap.

The proper correction for this was said to be for the guest to step gently but firmly on the exuberant hostess' back toes. The theory is that this will put a stop to the practice without breaking up the friendship—the dog is supposed to associate the pain not with the person causing it but with his own misbehavior.

I asked Sylvan to give Buddy the cure. So the next time she tackled him, off balance as he was, he shot out a well-shod foot and came down solidly on her left rear paw. Evidently Buddy had not read the rule book, for she immediately reacted as if Sylvan, not she, were responsible for her discomfort. Like a mother instructing a child "for his own good," she took Sylvan's wrist between her white teeth and looked warningly at him, as if to say, "That's enough now, you've gone too far!" Sylvan wasted no time withdrawing his foot, and Buddy rewarded him with a friendly lick, as if to say, "That's a good boy!" So that was the end of the antipounce lesson—and I think Sylvan learned a lot!

In the bosom of our family—or, perhaps I should say, "to the head of our family"—Buddy could do no wrong. When Mother complained that her sleeping on the bedspreads made for more laundering, Father's answer was, "Buy a washing machine!"

That showed Mother where she stood. A week later I found out where I stood. I was away from home for a few days and received the following letter. I quote it in its entirety: "Dear Morris: How is Buddy? Give her my love. Your Father."

I didn't really know how my Aunt Sadie felt about Buddy until the night we left the dog in her apartment while we went out to the theater. We returned rather late and found, to my horror, that Buddy had got hold of my aunt's new fifteen-dollar red feather hat and simply plucked it to pieces.

I expected all hell to break loose. Instead, to my surprise, Aunt Sadie exclaimed, "Why, Buddy, you smart thing!" as she gave the dog a big hug. "You knew that hat wasn't right for me. I did, too, but the salesgirl just talked me into buying it!"

Like Father, Aunt Sadie had suffered when I went from sightedness to helplessness and rejoiced when Buddy restored my self-sufficiency. If a fluff of scattered red feathers would add to that dog's happiness, Aunt Sadie thought nothing of providing the hat.

Another sister of my mother's, my Aunt Goldie, who "Before Buddy" had read to me nearly every Friday night, unfortunately was afraid of dogs and expected me to put Buddy outside when she arrived that first Friday, book in hand. I said I did not mind taking Buddy to the yard, but was afraid that Aunt Goldie might find it a little chilly reading out there!

She could not overcome her fear and refused to enter the house. Her own weakness infuriated her, so she determined to break herself of it by—excuse the expression—the hair of the dog. She bought a puppy for herself, and, like so many people who have a pet for the first time, she doted on hers. She became fonder of him than anyone else in the whole Frank family. Buddy was second in her affections. We humans, far from leading a dog's life, found ourselves way down at the bottom of her list.

These were the days of prohibition. One night about fifteen of us were in a speak-easy where someone objected to the dog, so we put her up at the table with us and treated her as a person. Every time we had a round of drinks, she had a slug of milk. The sight of this beautiful, dignified German shepherd sitting up on the chair with her paws primly on the table while she daintily drank her drink melted all feeling against her and soon we were all one big more-than-happy family.

When we left, I was tight. Buddy guided me as usual as long as we were on the sidewalk, but she refused to cross the street with me in my condition. She waited until someone came along to lend me an arm to help steady myself.

It was a wonder Buddy was not forced to look out for her master more often. Not that I had any tendency to take to drink. It was because of a job the fellows gave me. I became official taster of bathtub gin. The theory was that if it turned out to be poisonous, at least I would not go blind.

Each of the boys I grew up with now has a copy of the etching of Buddy, done by Mrs. C. Thurber. It has a prominent place in their offices or homes. When they speak of her, it is as of someone who is part of them, with the same love and affection that I feel for her.

Once, long ago, I had a quarrel with one of these good friends of Buddy's and mine. The next day we met him on the street. Buddy, with her usual cordiality, quickly moved over toward him, the way she did when she wanted to tell me, "Here comes a friend of ours." But he brushed by without speaking. I guessed who it was and also refused to break the silence.

After three days of this passing and ignoring each other, Buddy walked over, stopped right in front of him, put herself at "sit" without any command. She was plainly saying, "Will you two quit being fools and make up?"

We had to laugh. We admitted that Buddy showed better sense than we had, and we have been very close to each other ever since.

With special permission we rode the West End streetcar. Buddy delighted passengers by knowing our home stop. Even at midnight, when pitch blackness outside shut off all landmarks from her view, shortly before we reached our station she would rise from where she stretched beside the motorman, shake herself, and come back for me. Everyone was greatly amused. I would hear, "Watch the dog. See if she knows when to get off." Her "intuition" astonished them.

Being blind and alert to sounds, I learned how she did it. I noticed that just before our stop the car wheels made a special click-click sound, passing over a dead switch. When she heard this, she got up. Buddy had kept so many secrets for me, however, that until now I never gave away this one of hers.

It did not take long for Buddy's exploits to become the talk of the town. Her reputation preceded her everywhere. Once when we started to cross a street, a little eight-year-old boy asked me if I would take his hand and help him across.

Of course I was delighted, and when we reached the other side, I said, "Here we are, Sonny. And now will you tell me why you asked a blind man for help rather than someone who can see?"

"I know all about this dog," he replied, "and I knew that if I was with her, I'd be safe."

All Nashville took Buddy to its heart. The local kennel-club officials asked me to enter her in a dog show, and advertised her appearance. I should never have agreed. She had eaten at many of the best tables in the city and been fed by so many people, including my own father, who took advantage of my blindness to pamper her, that she was far too fat. And, despite my daily currying, she was completely out of coat when it came to competition with show dogs. The judge, an authority from a nearby state, rightly awarded the prize to another German shepherd.

But he had not reckoned with Buddy's home-town fans. The crowd, many of whom had come just to see her, were perhaps not experts when it came to professionally conducted dog shows, but they very well understood that Buddy was the smartest animal ever to hit Nashville. When she was not awarded the blue ribbon, a chorus of boos assailed the decision.

Someone explained her popularity to the bewildered judge, who was a man of resource. Recalling Buddy to the ring, he solemnly presented her with a special trophy as "Best *Imported* Bitch," to the deafening applause of her loyal friends.

Sometime later, when a newsreel was taken of Buddy at work, the Paramount marquee announced in big lights, "Buddy, Seeing Eye Dog," and in smaller ones underneath, "Also, Greta Garbo in *Camille*." Nashville knew a great star when it saw one. I didn't even get billing.

Speaking of the movies, Buddy and I went quite often. In the theater she lay quietly with her head under my seat and the rest of her stretched under the neighboring places in the same row. People usually did not know she was there. One night I reached down and gave her a nice pat and she wagged her tail. A lady who was sitting two seats away immediately complained to the usher, "Someone is tickling my leg!"

I felt that silence, not honesty, was the best policy at that moment. Buddy and I made our escape as soon as the commotion died down. After all, who cares to see a picture all the way through?

I was pleased that my insurance business was going well. As a matter of fact, like Buddy, it was growing by leaps and bounds. Mr. Pollard, my boss, picked us up in the morning.

Buddy would wait eagerly to hear his car come round the corner, and I must say, I think that if she had had two less feet, she would have made a wonderful public-relations executive. She always greeted Mr. P. as enthusiastically as if he were one of my "prospects" all ready to sign on the dotted line.

I no longer had trouble getting to talk to potential clients. They gave no secret signals to my guide to dodge my visit. My "victims" welcomed me. They were eager to ask about Buddy and watch her work. When word went in to a vice-president that Mr. Frank and his dog were here, the answer was a cordial, "Tell them to come in. Come right on in, Morris!"

So, again thanks to Buddy, I was leading a full life. I had friends, I was getting an education, and I was earning my own living. We had made solid progress in proving that dogs could be liberators in the fight against dependence.

My blindness was still with me, of course. But I had accepted that. What I had never accepted were the recurring mortifications like tripping over a tricycle and overhearing someone say, "Isn't that pitiful!"

I could hardly bear wanting to visit a friend and not wanting to ask anyone to take me. It was agony for me to go downtown with someone who would stand me on a corner "for just a minute" while they went on an errand that turned out to consume three quarters of an hour. As wonderful as friends and family were, it did mean waiting.

I think the worst was the falling—perhaps over a chair, or even just a couple of steps—and then trying to assure people I was not hurt. I wasn't, physically, but everything inside hurt.

These distressing evidences of my helplessness were now gone. In their place Buddy had brought me freedom, companionship, affection, and self-respect.

Chapter 5

AS THE newspaper and magazine stories and pictures about Buddy spread all over the country, many fellow blind wrote to me. One touching letter came from the Reverend R. A. Blair, a clergyman who had lost his sight three years previously as the result of an attack of malaria.

"I can read Braille and can write on the typewriter, as I am doing now," he wrote, "but I cannot visit my flock. My wife, who took me on calls at first, is now an invalid, bedridden for over a year and a half. My daughter is a cripple from infantile paralysis and so cannot help me to get around. Thus I am badly impeded in my work. When I heard your story read, I wondered if there would be any chance of getting help. If I only had a dog to take me about my parish, that would overcome about the only handicap I now suffer from blindness."

What spirit! Here was just the kind of stout-hearted person I was eager to assist. This minister was as wise and well informed now as he was before he became blind. He did not lose his rich knowledge of the Scriptures when he lost his sight. He might conceivably preach an even better sermon, since he had a deeper understanding of human suffering.

The one indispensable part of his duties he could not perform was to call on his parishioners. Without constant contact with them, he could not be the confidant and counselor his ministry demanded. Through no fault of his own, he was not doing his full job. Yet all he really needed to complete a full cycle of usefulness was to be able to move freely about his parish. I could picture his state of mind. What wouldn't a dog like Buddy mean to him!

A special delivery came from a lady in California who implored that she be given training and a guide dog. Two doctors, one in Savannah, Georgia, the other in Monmouth, Illinois, urgently asked for help. Local letters streamed in from Nashville and from all over Tennessee. I wrote to Mrs. Eustis about each case. Her answer bore the refrain, "I am still as convinced as you are of the great need for the work we can do. These individual appeals strengthen that belief."

My own conviction that the time to start our school was *right now* burst on me one September day when I was headed to the post office, a briefcase bulging with appeals that came from coast to coast.

As Buddy and I paused for a second at a busy corner before we plunged into the maelstrom of traffic, I heard the tapping of a blind man's cane as he stood at the curb and waited for some passing stranger charitably to take him across. We realized then and there we could never be happy until we had opened the school that would lead to self-respect for the many who were shuffling up to corners and standing there, objects of pity.

Things moved fast after that. Mrs. Eustis replied to my letter urging as-soon-as-possible action with very good news: Jack was progressing very well at Fortunate Fields with his teaching of instructors. One in particular would make a first-rate assistant for Jack.

"Surprisingly, she's a girl!" wrote Mrs. Eustis. "She's not more than twenty, has been a special family friend for years. Her name is Adelaide Clifford and, fortunately for us, unlike so many of her contemporaries, who are 'horse crazy,' Adelaide is 'dog crazy.' Jack thinks she has a genius for the work.

"Jack is also showing his own usual skill with the dogs," she continued. "He has two, Tata and Gala, who are almost human in their responses."

The best part of her letter Mrs. Eustis saved for the last. She thought I could safely set up beginning classes for February. "Jack will arrive sometime before that—we can't tell yet the exact date—expect him when you see him! I will follow after him as soon as I can arrange my affairs here at Fortunate Fields."

Very early on a cold morning in late December, Buddy and I left my house and started for the streetcar-loading platform. Suddenly, for no apparent reason, Buddy stopped in her tracks. I strained my ears to try to discover what it was that had turned her into a seeming statue. For a minute all was silence, then I heard what seemed to be familiar footsteps walking ahead of us. They rang out on the frozen sidewalks in a well-remembered staccato. My heart pounding, I called out, "Jack!" but no one answered. The one making the sound of the footsteps walked on. We followed for another block, then I cried again, "Jack!" Still no reply.

Finally I said, "You might as well admit you're there. You may be able to fool me, but you can't trick Buddy. Her head is up in that alert way that always meant 'Jack' in Switzerland. It can't be anyone but you!"

With that, Jack's hearty laugh pealed out on the crisp air. Then came that positive footstep toward us, a firm handclasp, a friendly hand gripping on my shoulder. Jack's first words were to Buddy. He patted her and said warmly, "Well, congratulations, old girl, you got us here!" And, to me, "Now, Morris, it's time to get to work."

We opened a small office, nine feet by ten, in the city. There we carried on the business of setting up schedules for classes, arranging housing for students, figuring expenses, dickering with kennel suppliers, and answering the ever-mounting mountains of mail that continued to pour in. The remarkable Miss Clifford arrived from Switzerland and was invaluable in taking care of the thousand and one details that would have swamped us otherwise.

Away from the center of town we rented an old broken-down house which we converted into kennels, boarding up the yard to make a quite spacious exercise area for the dogs.

Jack had brought with him the intelligent Tata and Gala, and little by little we secured others from breeders in various parts of the country. Only a few measured up to Jack's rigorous standards and were actually turned into finished guide dogs.

One promising beginner that failed was highly educable except in a single particular: no matter how much you corrected her, if anyone stepped on her tail, she could not help growling or barking in protest. As her blind master would be likely to tread on her inadvertently many times, the guide dog must understand that this is merely an occupational hazard which she must face with stoicism. A snarling, yelping animal is not pleasant company for her charge, and she would be bound to excite public distrust of our whole Seeing Eye establishment, so Jack reluctantly sold her.

W. H. "Willi" Ebeling, a breeder in Morristown, New Jersey, was a first-rate source of supply. He and Jack, in their mutual enthusiasm for the highest type of German shepherd, hit it off so well that Willi was persuaded to uproot himself and join us in Nashville, where his skill and devotion to our project made him an indispensable member of our staff. He soon became "Uncle" to all of us.

Things were beginning to hum by the time we welcomed Mrs. Eustis in January. We had overcome some initial difficulties and only waited her command, "Forward!" Everything seemed to be in order for our establishment as a bona-fide educational institution.

We incorporated The Seeing Eye under the laws of Tennessee as an organization "for the training and education of dogs as guides for the blind and for the training and education of men and women without sight in the use of the dogs." We were to be a nonprofit enterprise, with Mrs. Eustis as president and me as managing director.

We had three "angel" friends who pledged twenty-five hundred dollars apiece for three years to help defray operating expenses. Other than that, Mrs. Eustis, enthusiastically dedicated to our cause, cheerfully and generously offered the resources of her own checkbook against the onslaught of bills already coming in.

We opened the doors of our school exactly one year and three months after I read that blessed article and was fired with the dream of bringing guide dogs to America.

Our first class, starting in February, was filled to capacity and taxed our resources to the utmost. It consisted of two pupils, Dr. Raymond Harris of Savannah and Dr. Howard Buchanan of Monmouth, who had written us such compelling letters. These two physicians absorbed our full quota of guide dogs, the imported Tata and Gala—the only ones trained to the height of perfection Jack required before he ever trusted a dog with the responsibility of being a blind man's eyes.

Simultaneously, while these first pupils were learning to negotiate traffic and avoid obstacles, other dogs were being prepared for our second group of students, scheduled to arrive for their instruction in March.

Jack, a noted geneticist, was also a remarkable trainer. Merely to talk with him an hour was to marvel at his knowledge of all living creatures. Before taking up duties with Mrs. Eustis, he had worked with circus animals—horses, elephants, dogs, and lions. Once told that no one had ever succeeded in coaching a camel to walk backwards, he picked up the challenge and disciplined three dromedaries to do the impossible—in unison!

Jack and Willi devoted three months to readying each dog we intended to use. We kept to German shepherds because of their extraordinary intelligence, stamina, and fidelity, and found that young females, about fourteen months old, were most cooperative.

The first step of her "kindergarten" training was to teach her to be absolutely housebroken. The second step is obedience training and then teaching her that when she is in harness she is at *work*. At that time she must absolutely ignore distractions such as other dogs or bold tomcats that challenge her attention. In her hours of play she can chase all the squirrels she likes, but the minute the harness goes on, that leather strapping is the same as a "Do Not Disturb" sign that must be honored.

This lesson is an education in itself and of itself starts the intelligent dog thinking. She learns that no matter what her own feelings are, she is never to desert her master to fight or play.

She is then ready to graduate to her next class—obedience exercises. She learns to go forward, turn right and left, sit and lie down. She also learns to fetch and to pick up anything her master might drop. All of the dogs become expert retrievers. They could pick up collar buttons and even coins in their mouths by turning their heads sideways to the floor. Occasionally one would astonish Jack by retrieving an object, say a key, he did not even realize he had lost.

The dog passed gradually from the lower to the higher grades of work and was not given advanced problems before she had mastered the simple ones. Her first days in harness were spent in learning to come to a complete "sit," at every curb, so that her master would know that the block was finished, get his bearings, and decide whether to give the command "Forward!" or "Right!" or "Left!"

Jack spent long hours patiently rehearsing this basic exercise, then would allow the dog to make the mistake of starting to cross a street without sitting and waiting for his command. The minute that happened, Jack would elaborately stumble and jerk the harness exactly as a blind man would. That was not much fun for the dog, and her common-sense reaction soon eliminated all trial and error connected with this part of her curriculum.

All training was accompanied with immediate praise— "That's a good girl!" for work done correctly and with dispatch. How the dogs cringed when they had to be told "Phooey!" for making mistakes!

A spectacular feature of this period of the training was teaching the dog to avoid overhanging obstacles under which she herself could easily pass but which would injure her taller companion. Jack would approach an awning so low-slung that it would hit him in the face if he were to run into it. He would bang it vigorously with his stick, knowing the noise would impress the sensitive dog. He would then walk her around the obstacle, and immediately return to it again. Unless she evaded it this time, he would give her a firm correction and they would try it several times more. When she finally realized what was expected of her, Jack patted and praised her. In time she progressed to where she made automatic detours for all overhanging objects like a *good* girl.

After a dog was taught obedience, Jack as carefully taught her intelligent disobedience—if carrying out a command would be dangerous to her master. The development of this power of discretion was the higher mathematics of her course of education. Jack wanted to be positive that if the command "Forward!" was given and the dog saw a car bearing down on them, she would refuse to move or would pull her charge backward.

He believed that a dog must obey perfectly yet never function as a machine; she must be given freedom to use her intelligence and initiative. Our dogs, then, learned to obey and yet be ready to disobey intelligently if, for instance, an irresponsible driver jumped a red light, or if some other sudden violence threatened. As Jack knew from experience in Europe, many a blind man has given an order in the face of unseen danger and had his life saved when his guide refused to budge or even threw herself down, pressing back against his legs to protect him.

For the dog's final examination Jack or Uncle Willi actually put on a blindfold and let the dog lead him through traffic. Relying only on her own judgment, the apt pupil took her erstwhile instructor through heavy traffic. At busy corners she would stop to let cars that had made a legitimate turn go by, or, if the situation called for it, hurry him across if the automobiles slowed down for them. Sure-footed, the guides threaded their way through thronged sidewalks without so much as brushing fellow pedestrians. They led their pretend-blind charges under archways, around mailboxes, and through revolving doors as smoothly as if they were traveling on ball bearings.

Conscientious to the extreme, Jack put a guide dog through countless tests until he had perfect faith in her judgment and implicit confidence that she was ready to graduate. Only then did he take off his blindfold, tell the dog she was more than a good girl—she was a *perfect* girl; only then was she given the diploma which declared her deserving to be trusted with the great responsibility of being a blind man's eyes.

We had five guide dogs ready for our March class and had facilities to more than double the first month's enrollment of our "student body." The carefully chosen pupils were a lady who came to us all the way from Berkeley, California; Earl Pendleton of Indian Springs, Tennessee; E. A. Rogers and Sidney Sweeney of Nashville; and Dr. R. A. Blair, the Pennsylvania minister who longed to be able to independently pay calls on his parishioners.

Their actual instruction began with a pep talk which Jack delivered with enthusiasm.

"We are glad to have you here, and you are lucky to be with us," he said. "You have been chosen from hundreds of applicants. You will find the training hard, but you will find it immeasurably rewarding. It may possibly be a matter of life and death to you.

"I remember one winter day in the Potsdamer Platz when a young blind girl fell in the middle of the icy square. Her guide dog quickly took her by the coat collar and dragged her to the safety of the sidewalk. We don't expect that to happen to any of you, but from our experience we know your dog is going to be a lifesaver in many ways."

Before the students were given their dogs, each was instructed individually in the use of the harness handle. Jack led them around by it as if he were the actual guide dog. He padded straight ahead with them in tow, then wheeled unexpectedly to right or left. "Take a firm grip. Not too hard, not too loose—just steady and firm. That handle's the means of communication between you and your dog. In time you'll learn to know just what it is saying."

Jack kept up a steady stream of talk as he demonstrated the feel of the pull in various directions. "It's like learning to tune a radio dial. The signals are fuzzy at first, but with a little practice and experience they'll come in loud and clear and unmistakable.

"Don't try to make your dog go one way or another by twisting her harness. It's not a rein. Don't try to lead her; let

Morris Frank and his first Seeing Eye dog, Buddy (1931).

Jack Humphrey, a geneticist, went to Potsdam, Germany, to learn the highly specialized technique of training dog guides. He had trained Buddy, and Morris Frank was his first human pupil.

Dorothy Harrison Eustis, with three German shepherds, the breed she raised and trained for police and Red Cross work, on her estate in the Swiss Alps. As a result of a letter from Mr. Frank requesting a dog guide, she began training these dogs for the blind.

After Morris arrived in Switzerland, getting acquainted was the first step. Mrs. Eustis and Mr. Humphrey, above, introduced the 20-year-old boy to his dog, and the intensive training began. Buddy I, below, was the sensitive, alert, affectionate dog that restored Morris Frank's confidence and led him back to life—a new, productive life.

The return trip, with Buddy, was a thrilling experience in independence, and a great contrast to the voyage over. This time Morris did not feel as if he were an American Express parcel, to be handled with care. In Nashville, below, surprised citizens paused in their daily activity to watch Morris and Buddy move about the city freely; but they soon came to accept the two as a familiar sight.

The loneliness, the timidity and dejection so apparent in the young boy of 20 have disappeared as the man of today strides through life with head up and shoulders back.

Believe it or not, these five hungry pups are future dog guides for the blind. About ten weeks after birth they leave the 100-acre Breeding Farm and are taken to 4-H Club homes, where they are given a normal, happy home life for about a year.

New puppies are welcomed to a 4-H Club farm and a mature pup bids
farewell to her playmates. She is now ready to begin her schooling. School-
days, for both dog guides and their blind masters, are spent at The Seeing
Eye headquarters, formerly a 50-acre estate, in Morristown, New Jersey.

Photos by Iris Ve

Before she meets her blind master, each dog works with a sighted trainer for three months in Morristown. At top, this canine student gains practical experience with city traffic. For one month the blind student receives individual instruction with his dog under the close supervision of the dog's trainer. The boxer, in bottom picture, guides her master around an open manhole as the instructor keeps a close watch on things.

Photos by Iris Veit

The handicapped are no longer disinherited, as these pictures show. Employed as a receptionist, the blind man at top, familiar with the building, gives clear directions and information to a sighted person. In another occupational group, farmers can benefit from guide dogs' adaptability. Despite the distractions of farm animals and small boys, the dog guides her master through the daily chores.

Blind people no longer need be occupational risks. A factory worker carries on at his job while his dog sits quietly out of the way.

Photo by Iris Veit

Photo by Iris Veit

Many offices employ blind typists, like this one, who transcribe from dictating machines.

Buddy II succeeded Morris Frank's first dog, who died in 1938, after ten years of faithful duty. The name "Buddy" is reserved for Mr. Frank's Seeing Eye dogs.

In 1947 Morris Frank and Buddy II met with President Truman and the Committee on "National Employ the Physically Handicapped Week."

Morris Frank and Buddy travel all over the country, visiting graduates and prospective students and giving lectures and demonstrations. Here, in a dramatic display of the effective relationship between dog and master, Buddy guides Mr. Frank through the unfamiliar streets of Vancouver, B.C.

Dog guides and their blind masters cross intersections with more ease and safety than many sighted people. Mr. Frank and Buddy III are a well-known pair in Morristown. On the way to work, below, both exchange friendly greetings with the townspeople.

Photos by Alvina Murphy

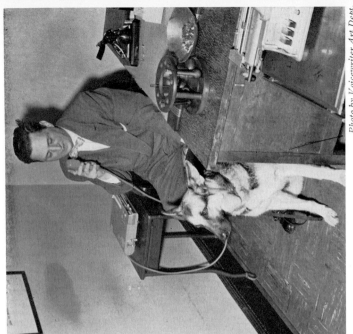

Photo by Voicewriter Art Dept.

At his insurance office in Morristown, Morris Frank is hard at work, while Buddy, ever alert, awaits his next command.

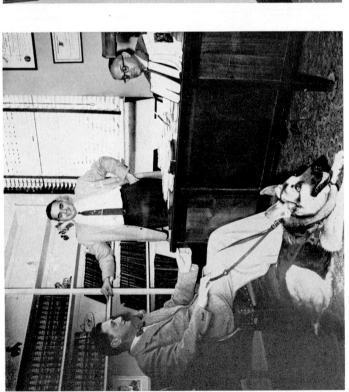

Photo by Alvina Murphy

The insurance business demands a regular round of visits to clients. Here, Buddy is relaxing while Morris Frank talks shop.

The sighted and the blind alike participate in the day-to-day living that includes such things as purchasing a Christmas wreath for the front door.

Photo by Alvina Murphy

Photo by Alvina Murphy

Morris often helps out with such household tasks as shopping.

Photo by Iris Veit

An integral part of the Frank household, Buddy III receives equally affectionate attention from Morris and his wife, Lois.

Devotion, intelligence, responsiveness: these are the qualities that make Buddy III a true representative of The Seeing Eye.

Photo by Iris Veit

her lead you! Now," Jack ordered, "command me, and praise me if I get it right!"

Only after they were letter-perfect in the intonation of their directional orders and their unvarying, enthusiastic words of reward for their mythical dog, were they ready to meet their own guide dogs to be.

At that time Jack told the students, who were tense with anticipation: "This dog has been minutely analyzed to be sure that her character and temperament will match your own. She has been brought up to know that you are her responsibility. Her whole life has been a preparation to assure that trust. She lives only to be your eyes, and asks in return only that you love her and give her your companionship.

"But you must remember," he cautioned, "she does not belong to you—you belong to her. You cannot force her to obey you; you can only make her love you so that she will want to do so.

"And, at last," Jack would say, dramatically, "here is the one destined to be the most important woman in your life!"

This was a red-letter day in the student's life—when he was introduced to his dog. "Remember," Jack warned, "she guides you, but you must tell her where to go. You're the brains, she's the eyes—it's a fifty-fifty proposition."

Hundreds of hours of concentration later, that fifty-fifty proposition had developed to 100 per cent success. The students had overcome the discomfort of aching shoulders and leg muscles, and, what was worse, the agony of recurring fears of failure that shadowed their joys and accomplishment.

In three weeks they graduated.

They had come to Seeing Eye hesitantly and timidly, shuffling and feeling their way along. They strode briskly away from our doors with heads up—reborn human beings. It was hard to believe they were really blind.

As each month brought new students and eager classes, plain-spoken Jack developed detailed instructions so our trainees would be prepared for every phase of their lives with their dogs.

"Gentlemen," he would say early in the course, "you must never fail in your duty to see that your dog has a regular time to answer the call of nature. At no other times except the correct and precise times must you give her freedom for that purpose. We have done our part in training her in this respect. Now it's up to you to be sure she does not break training.

"The second fundamental thing for you to remember is that she has been trained to be your eyes *at all times*. When she is in harness, do not let her sniff at hydrants when she pleases. She cannot be off attending to her love life when you need to be taken across the street."

Most students tried to carry out Jack's instructions to the letter. His insistence on their complimenting their dogs for good work soon required no insistence. The coveted "That's a good girl" came spontaneously from grateful hearts. I do recall, however, one blustery fellow who, no matter how often he was reminded, still had to be constantly exhorted, "Praise your dog! Reward your dog!" In his concentration he just did not seem to be able to remember to give her the affection she needed.

He kept shouting at his guide, yanking her off her feet, never giving her a pat or an encouraging word. Jack warned him that the dog would never put her heart in her work unless she felt loved, but his words were in vain.

One morning this student and his dog were walking briskly along a street. Jack, following them, was surprised to see the dog head straight for a fire hydrant. Was she going to break all rules of training and pause to sniff the hydrant? No! She had just decided to take the matter of her master's education into her own capable hands. Without letting up her fast clip, she just grazed the iron hydrant, leading her undemonstrative master to hit it full force with both knees. Needless to say, he learned his lesson the hard way and mended his ways.

The incident was a boon to future training. When Jack told a class to reward the dog with praise, and then related this grim example as a warning, they remembered with ease that love conquers all.

As time went on, we began to take in some newly-blind students. Their problems were different from those who had lived with the fact of blindness for some time.

We tried to encourage them with the right approach to their recent loss of sight so that they could adjust to it more easily. Our goal was to help them remain active, normal, contributing members of their communities. Often these young men and women needed more than our technical training and talk.

We wanted to give them confidence and a feeling of equality with those who see.

One place they needed help was at the dining table. It is quite simple and natural to find one's mouth, even when blind, but it is another story to be sure there is food on one's fork to put in it after the "lift" has been made successfully. Nothing makes a person feel more foolish than carefully to raise a fork to his mouth and get nothing but a biteful of silver.

We taught them the trick of thinking of their plates as clock faces. They would locate a serving of meat, say, at figure six, potatoes at nine. It was wonderful to see a boy's sense of humor resurge with his new self-reliance. One, delighted at his prowess, convulsed his classmates with, "I do believe I'll have another bite of those three o'clock beans" and, "Did you ever taste such delicious half-past seven carrots?"

Another little tip to further their confidence also had to do with the clock, or rather with their watches. Sometimes time passes slowly for the blind, and we saved them the embarrassment of having to ask over and over again, "Please, what time is it?" They know that this recurring question becomes as annoying as a child's continual "Are we almost there?" on a long trip. We showed them watches made for the blind, with raised dots marking the hours.

Many students told us we helped them in their personal relationships by reminding them about turning light switches on and off. Of course a blind person can see just as well after the sun goes down as he could before, but it is bad "public relations" for them to be caught doing it. It shocks a sighted person to enter a room to find a blind one reading a Braille book or listening to the radio. There is something eerie about it.

"Since you pointed out the 'Let there be light' policy," said one of the boys, "I don't even listen to records after sundown without turning on the lamps. It does make me feel more cheerful and normal, and I know it makes my parents and friends more comfortable."

One morning as I was having read to me the mail that brought urgent requests for admission from all over the country, we came upon a letter from Parnassus, Pennsylvania. It was from Dr. Blair, alumnus of our March class. He sent us greetings from Dot, the beautiful German shepherd he had already come to love so much, and told us other news.

"When I first returned," he wrote, "I heard that among a few of my flock there was some question as to the propriety of Dot's lying in the pulpit while I preached. The next Sunday I turned to Matthew for my text. 'The Lord hath need of them,' I pointedly expounded. The reaction was wonderful. After that, Dot was welcomed wholeheartedly. I suppose the reasoning in the pews was, 'Well, if the Lord needs them, who are we to complain about the one that means so much to Dr. Blair?' "

The minister closed his letter with, "I am sure it is due to Dot, in great measure, that our church membership has steadily increased. She is my beloved companion on visits to my parishioners. She is so eager, so full of life that if she had her way, we would be paying calls all the time. I must continually hold her back," concluded Dr. Blair, "for now that I've found them, I certainly don't want to wear out my eyes!"

Chapter 6

⊂⊂⊂⊂⊂⊂⊂

*M*UCH as we all loved my home town, Nashville was not the ideal location for a Seeing Eye training school. The long summer season was oppressively hot. After two trips in the stifling heat of some days, when pavements and asphalt roads burned through shoe leather, dogs and students alike were sweltering and exhausted. Ideally we needed to be in the country, with a city nearby for practice runs.

Our thoughts turned to the cooler Atlantic Coast. Mrs. Eustis was an Easterner, as were many other wealthy folk whose financial support we needed. Then, too, there were, naturally, more blind to be helped in the metropolitan areas; people could reach us more easily if we established ourselves nearer to them.

As we looked around for a place to leap, we found a spot to land, at least temporarily. Uncle Willi Ebeling generously offered us the use of the facilities of his country place by Lake Openaka, six miles from Morristown, New Jersey.

So in the spring of 1929, like the camel that nosed into the Arab's tent, our organization moved in with Uncle Willi and Mrs. Ebeling and appropriated most of their quarters. Our instructors occupied their gate house, our dogs their kennels, while Mrs. Eustis, Jack, and I, as well as others of our growing staff, swarmed into the house proper practically every weekend. The Ebelings, however, did not complain of the crowding. They loved the excitement of helping us plan and grow. Both of them meant a great deal to me; they treated me as if I were their son, and, to me, their place was home.

Here we were joined by Billy Debetaz, the energetic French-Swiss instructor who had completed his training at Fortunate Fields. He, at twenty-three, was wiry and as full of bounding energy as the animals under his command. Each morning he loaded the dogs and his assistants into a Ford truck and hauled them into Morristown, whose streets were our new practice pavements.

Our situation had serious disadvantages. Students had to be billeted in hotels or boarding houses, so did not have contact with the staff except during strictly working hours. But we tried to solve each day's problems as they arose and put all of our energies into the classes.

All the time we were "making do," Mrs. Eustis was quietly talking to real-estate dealers. She had dedicated herself completely to our Seeing Eye work, as her pleasure in life was to help people who first indicated a burning desire to help themselves. One morning in August, 1931, she telephoned us to meet her at a place three miles from Morristown. "I have something to show you," she promised.

Uncle Willi and I, following her directions, turned off the highway onto the tree-lined driveway of an imposing piece of property. It was surrounded by green lawns and wooded acreage.

"It's a mansion!" exclaimed Uncle Willi.

"*Descendez-vous*, gentlemen, and welcome to our new home!" Mrs. Eustis greeted us.

We were elated. We inspected every nook, closet, and corner of the three-story Victorian house. The Boss was as pleased with our reaction as if she had hammered every nail in it herself. "There's plenty of room on the first floor for all the office

space we'll need for years to come!" she exclaimed enthusiastically. "And after that," she went on, her excitement carrying her away, "we'll screen in the porch for hundreds and
thousands of typewriters and filing cabinets!"

We made a tour of the fifty-six-acre estate, our delight in its
possibilities for us mounting with every step. It had everything
we needed for a completely integrated dog-training and stu-
dent-instructing school. Two buildings on the spacious grounds
could be converted into excellent kennels, opening onto big
lawns, front and back, for exercise and education of the dogs.
Best of all, there were plenty of kitchen and dining facilities
and bedrooms for a student dormitory. We could now give
pupils a four-week course crammed with valuable pointers
about dining, dressing, grooming, and recreation that should
make their daily living infinitely easier and more pleasant.

"The property is ours, lock, stock and barrel," Mrs. Eustis
told us. "And I think I know some friends who'll be glad to
help us with expenses. Let's make out a class schedule and
plan our first menu for the new dining room, right now!"

We had built a firm foundation since that auspicious home-
coming day that Buddy led me down the gangplank of that
transatlantic liner to face that first battery of hard-boiled newspaper men and photographers. We had given new hope to
fifty men and women, and not a single one at the school had
ever had a serious accident. Observers of our work were saying
that The Seeing Eye had made the greatest contribution since
Braille toward lightening the burden of blindness. Already we
had a list of several hundred applicants impatiently awaiting
the time when we could enroll them.

Now we were ready to go forward to a greater future. To
help meet the increasing demands upon us, Mrs. Eustis asked
Jack to go to Vevey, close her establishment there and bring
the dogs in training to Morristown.

With the establishment of permanent headquarters, I

worked harder than ever, devoting every waking minute to The Seeing Eye. Experienced, able people joined us, some informally, as consultants, others as members of the staff, but all for the love of it, whether paid or not. Mervin Sinclair, head of the Pennsylvania State Council for the Blind, himself had a Seeing Eye dog, Kara.

Broun, chief of the Employment Bureau of New York State; Mary Dranga Campbell, who knew more about problems of the blind than anyone else I had ever met; and Ibby Hutchinson, who came on the staff, were among the group.

Many is the long but rewarding hour we spent thrashing out the plans, policies, and problems of our movement.

One of the most vexing difficulties was that of getting dogs. Uncle Willi's kennels were long ago stripped as a source of supply, and he was finding it almost impossible to collect others with temperament suitable for the work. We required very important special characteristics. The dog selected must be neither too shy nor too aggressive. She must be intelligent, calm, and of friendly disposition. When Uncle Willi found such a paragon, she still had to go through many tests before we dared take her for training. For instance, to test her nerves and stability Uncle Willi would unexpectedly explode a firecracker almost under her nose. A dog likely to be thrown into panic by any loud noise or by the sudden backfire of an automobile could not be depended upon to keep her head and guard the safety of a blind master in an emergency.

The real bottleneck preventing rapid expansion, however, was lack of good instructors. Debetaz, of course, was first rate. He fulfilled the promise in America that the Boss had observed on her estate in Vevey. His make-up, like Jack's, contained all the ingredients that go into making a successful trainer: physical stamina, mental alertness, a sense of humor, and the will to do all the hard work necessary to "make a pair of eyes."

In Europe they took three to five years to train an instructor. Being mass-minded Americans, we thought we would be able to speed up this system and would soon be turning trainers out in assembly-line time.

It did not work out that way. The instructor's job is two-fold: he must be able and willing not only to train the dogs but to teach the blind to use them. Some aspirants would excel at one part of the work, some at the other; those who did both equally well were rare.

I recall one man who was good with dogs and who liked his blind pupils. But the job just called for more strength than he could muster. After walking fourteen to fifteen miles a day, tense every minute to see that the student in his care learned to act with full confidence yet was guarded against danger, he was mentally and physically exhausted. We were sorry when he gave up, but could see that the nervous strain was just too great for him.

Certain candidates who worked out very well under close supervision failed under the wear and tear of being on their own initiative. One promising young fellow worked himself into a complete mental breakdown. Many instructors came and went; a few marvelous ones stayed.

Some policies developed as the result of bitter experience. Our working expenses were high. There were dogs and rations to be bought, salaries to be paid, supplies and equipment to be purchased. We figured it cost us just about fifteen hundred dollars to give a student the four weeks' training course, including his board and lodging. As we definitely were not and did not ever mean to be a profitmaking organization, we set three hundred and seventy-five dollars as the price we would ask for a dog. That amount, only a fourth of the expense to us, included everything we offered—even to the provision of the dog's special-made leather harness.

At first we accepted the money from any civic group or club

that wanted to make a Seeing Eye dog their project. They would send us a check and designate a particular blind person from their community to receive the benefit of it.

We soon found out, however, that following this procedure was a mistake. Some clubs were exploiting the graduates and their dogs, using them to publicize their own "generosity."

In one case, for example, a service club in a Middle Western city collected three hundred and seventy-five dollars in donations and sent a blind musician to us for training. When he returned home, everywhere he went he overheard people saying, "Look, there goes the service-club dog." Every day of his life he was reminded that he was an object of charity. It got so he hated to go outside his house, even to go to work.

This was defeating our aim at Seeing Eye—to help ambitious blind men and women to become independent physically, mentally, and economically.

Another graduate of ours, a young lady in her twenties, called on me when I was in a Midwestern city on a speaking trip. She was miserable. An agency for the blind there had raised funds, made a contribution to us, and arranged for her to come to Morristown. Upon her return home she found that the woman director of the agency, without even discussing it with the girl, had scheduled public appearances for her all over the city. What is more, she insisted that her protégée keep the engagements—twenty-seven at the time she talked to me. At each assembly the embarrassed young blind girl was introduced as "the lucky miss to whom we gave the dog!"

It was my pleasure to return the agency's money and make it unmistakably clear to its female director that she could not exploit the blind in return for the payment of a paltry sum. The money was the least important part of the cost of their agonizing struggle for independence. Were they to be robbed of their dignity after all they had been through to gain it?

We made it a rule that all contributions had to be made

76

directly to The Seeing Eye and could not be tagged for any one person. We further decided that, to encourage his confidence and pride in himself, each student must pay for his own dog. We lowered the price to one hundred and fifty dollars, which it was believed almost anyone could meet over a period of years. A student could take as long as he needed—years, if necessary—to settle the account; but we wanted him never to feel beholden to anyone, not even ourselves, for his most precious possession. Upon death of a dog, a second costs only fifty dollars.

A young mother, Mary, in Milwaukee, was only one of our graduates who showed us that our decision was absolutely right. Despite her blindness she held down a job in a factory. She rose early every morning to make breakfast for herself, her baby, and the dog before leaving for work. She placed the baby in a two-wheeled stroller and, holding the guide dog's harness with her left hand, pulled the baby with her right. Six blocks they walked to the bus stop.

Just to board the bus was a major undertaking. She had to fold the stroller, hang it over her right arm, hold the baby securely in the same arm, keep a tight grip on the dog's harness with her left hand, and pay her fare at the same time.

She delivered the baby to a nursery where it was cared for during the day, then walked one mile to her job. The evening routine was the same, in reverse—to nursery and then home again to cook, feed the baby, clean the house, wash clothes, and get ready for the next morning.

"Mary," I said, "you know there are state and Federal funds available to mothers and children in cases like yours. Why don't you apply for assistance?"

Her answer made me very proud. "When I came to Seeing Eye and got Sara," she said, "I paid for her out of my own earnings. It was the first thing I ever earned. That gave me a feeling of self-respect. Just because things aren't going well for me right now, I'm not going to sacrifice that feeling. I've got Sara. I don't need charity."

A young blind piano tuner came to us at Morristown. He was determined to get from house to house to do his work without having to depend on any other person in the world. I do not remember any student who learned faster than Larry. He and his dog were "in tune" from the moment they were introduced to each other. They were a perfectly matched duet when they returned to his home town.

He had been back at work for a few weeks when a delegation from his Christian Endeavor Society called on him.

"Larry," the spokesman said, "we're proud of you and have collected one hundred and fifty dollars. We would like to give it to you to pay for your dog."

Larry was touched. "I appreciate your thoughtfulness more than I can say," he replied. "But I went to Morristown in order to be able *to pay my own way*. That includes everything, right from the beginning.

"As a matter of fact, Seeing Eye *requires* each student to assume his own obligation," he explained. "You can't get in unless you show you're willing to undertake the responsibility. That lets them know you're serious about wanting to fight for your independence."

"You won the fight, all right, Larry," one of his friends observed. "Since you got that dog, you almost need de-independentizing!"

Larry laughed. "Tell you what," he suggested. "Let's use the money to fix up the chairs in the C-E meeting hall. I've noticed—don't ask me how—that those prickly old wickerwork seats are just about gone. They could really stand a good job of recaning."

Some weeks later Larry was leaving a house where he had just tuned a piano when he heard a woman on the sidewalk say to her companion, "Here comes Larry—he's the blind boy who became a man and wouldn't take charity."

Overhearing that one remark was worth far more to Larry than the price of his dog—even had he paid for her in pure gold, which he often told me she was worth.

Chapter 7

⬤⬤⬤⬤⬤⬤⬤⬤

S OUR graduates returned home to become valued
members of their communities and as publicity about
our efforts permeated the country, we became better and
better known. The story of our little pioneer group seemed to
fascinate the public, and we received numerous requests for
a speaker to come and talk about the work of The Seeing Eye.
Many included offers of payment, and we needed the money.
What most of our correspondents really wanted was to see
Buddy in action, so Mrs. Eustis, whom we all now called
"Boss," decided that I should turn lecturer, accompanied, of
course, by the real star of our establishment.

So Buddy and I started traveling. I knew nothing of public speaking, but with her on the platform beside me, I was
confident that I would have an interested audience.

I shall never forget our first appearance. It was in Louisville,
Kentucky, before the International Lions Clubs, with seventy-
five hundred members present. Listening to the exciting rumble of so many voices, gradually getting louder, I began to
feel a little faint with nervousness. Buddy, on the other hand,
behaved as if she had been born in a theatrical trunk, one of
a backstage litter. As if to make up for my stage fright, her
stage presence was superb. She sat ramrod straight on her
haunches, her alert head high, and her intelligent eyes snapping with excitement.

79

At the close of the introduction, when Buddy heard the chairman speak my name and the huge audience applauded, she joined in the acclamation with a rousing round of barks. The crowd roared with delight. All this good will on both sides of the footlights settled my nerves and got me off to a fine start.

Before I launched into a description of how The Seeing Eye operates, I told them how glad I was to have the opportunity to tell them that the sighted person's attitude means everything to those who cannot see.

"Be natural with a blind person," I urged them, "in both your voice and bearing. Avoid pity. Don't express sympathy for him in his presence. Don't wait on him too much; let him use his own powers. Be cheerful but not falsely cheerful. Use the same expressions, 'to read,' 'to see,' that you did before your friend lost his sight.

"I myself never think of not being able 'to see' in the usual way. I believe in the ability to see with the mind's eye. I visualize the sun shining on white buildings, the green shutters, the trees and birds—sometimes I think I 'see' more than those who rush through life without *looking*.

"One of the most thrilling experiences I ever had was visiting a wonderful statue that Malvina Hoffman had created. She had fashioned a marble archer, his bow taut and arrow ready to fly. I touched the bow and with my fingers 'saw' the grain of the wood, even though it was chiseled of purest stone.

"That's what I mean when I say a man without his eyes can see. He can visualize to an extraordinary degree. You need not be afraid to ask him, 'Have you seen our friend Mary lately?' He will appreciate your not fumbling around and coming up with an unnatural word that makes him feel like a freak."

I could feel the *rapport* grow between the audience and

myself. It gave me confidence to describe our actual day-to-day work. They were most attentive and sympathetic. I felt I could tell that they were as proud as I when I concluded with, "—and now we have fourteen of these noble dogs dedicated to service."

Of course Buddy stole the show. We gave a demonstration of how we work together and she obeyed my commands with clockwork precision. She really rose to the occasion. The strangeness of the huge hall, the unfamiliarity of the stage, the unprecedented situation, with thousands of pairs of eyes intently focused on our every move, rattled her not one whit. As a matter of fact, the electric atmosphere seemed to stimulate her.

I wish Hollywood could have seen her! There is no doubt she deserved an Oscar for the best performance of the year.

They kept us in the auditorium for an hour after we had finished our scheduled talk. The questions fairly flew.

"But, Mr. Frank, I thought dogs were color-blind. How can they tell the difference between a stop and go light at a street corner?"

"Your dog does not have to know whether the signal is red or green," I explained. "Your own ears 'hear' the colors. On red you listen to the traffic going by against you; on green the flow is with you. It's up to you to give the correct command."

"But if you say, 'Forward!' " the questioner interposed, "and some car tries to beat a light, you're sure to get hit."

"Don't underestimate the dog," I reminded him. "She doesn't want to get killed any more than you do. If some stupid driver defies the traffic lights, the dog won't take a single step on 'Forward!' "

"But I thought you said she was obedient."

"She is, but not crazy. She won't execute foolish and dangerous commands that might hurt her and you, since you're holding her harness. If, for instance, you ordered her to jump off a roof, she would just back up and give you a silent 'Phooey!'—the same as she received when she was being trained in 'intelligent disobedience.' "

"Mr. Frank," another listener spoke up, "it still is not clear to me how the dogs know where the blind want to go. Aren't you likely to start out for church and end up at a poolroom?"

"No," I laughed, "there is no danger of that unless you yourself change your mind on the way. Your dog does not know your destination; she merely answers your directions, "Right!" or "Left!" or "Forward!" By these commands she takes her master where *he* wants to go."

"But isn't he apt to end up lost?"

"The blind person usually knows his own community. To get anywhere in it, he just counts the blocks and keeps track of the turns on the way to keep his sense of direction."

"What if you're in a strange city and don't know your way to a certain place?"

"Then you do as any other stranger does—ask directions. You'll be told, 'Four blocks straight ahead, then make a right turn and go on a block and a half,' for instance. All you have to do is give the commands and your dog guides you. When you think you are about there, you check on your position by asking someone for more information."

I recalled following this procedure once in Chicago. I thought I had kept careful count of the blocks we had traveled, but wasn't quite sure of where we were. When I asked a man where the People's Gas Building was, he replied, "What's the matter with you? Are you blind? You're standing right in front of it!" Before I could pick up my dog's harness and give her the command to go in, a young man came up to me and said, "I beg your pardon, sir, but where is the People's Gas Building?" I have to admit that I could not resist demanding, rather triumphantly, "What's the trouble? You blind? It's right in front of you!"

As I concluded, the audience generously applauded, Buddy barked again, and our first "lecture" ended in a roar of fun.

For Buddy and me this was the beginning of a career that took us into many states and to the speaking platforms of countless clubs and conventions. Early in our appearance Buddy made it quite clear that she was a guide dog, not a trick dog, and would put up with no foolishness. People, naturally curious to see how she worked, would ask me to let them suggest the commands, just to test her out. Perhaps they thought we had a prearranged routine that we used for demonstration purposes only, I don't know. Anyway, when I agreed to the trial, every doubter—nine times out of ten— would outline, "Forward!" then, "Right! Right! Right!" and we would end up right back where we started from. Buddy could see that this was leading nowhere, that the experiment was pointless, and after a time refused to negotiate the meaningless square.

One noontime a group asked me to have Buddy fetch my handkerchief, which she did. A few days later another audience wanted to see her do the same thing; then later a third asked her to execute the same trick. By this time Buddy could tell that I did not really need that blasted handkerchief and when I gave the command "Fetch!" she decided to illustrate once and for all that she was no vaudeville performer. She loped over to the piece of white linen that I had dropped ostentatiously to the floor and picked it up expertly with her teeth. She then proceeded deliberately to step on the trailing corners with her front paws and tear the handkerchief neatly in two. Then she carefully brought me the two separate parts. She had "fetched" for me, all right; as a matter of fact, she had given us all exactly twice as much as we had bargained for.

Our audiences always seemed to enjoy the "Q. and A." part

of our talks. The one query I could always depend on getting was: "How does a blind person go about getting a Seeing Eye dog?"

My answer was, "It's rather like the procedures connected with adopting a baby.

"First of all, the dog has been carefully selected—we know he is young and healthy, with quiet, steady nerves, and good character. Then the would-be master has to be just as carefully screened to insure he is fit to have the dog. Not all the blind are able to use a guide dog. We must choose a person who is mentally alert and neither too young nor too old.

"The man must be in good physical condition. The training period itself is strenuous; after that we must look out for the dog; we must be sure that he won't have to drag a load—his owner must be able to walk out in the world on his own two feet.

"Then comes another hurdle. We have numerous questionnaires we ask applicants to fill out. These help us decide which ones are *worthy* of a Seeing Eye dog. We want to provide them for men and women who have the desire to be actively employed or to participate in community activities. The ones who get the dogs are the men who tell us they want to go back to their productive work as teachers, lawyers, doctors, factory workers, or salesmen; or the women who want to go forward leading full lives as wives and mothers; or college students preparing for useful careers.

"At last we carefully study the answers to the questionnaires to gain insight into an applicant's temperament. These replies help us choose which of our dogs will be the right one for the master, and vice versa. Only when all qualifications, on all counts for both parties concerned, are met in full do we ask the applicant to come to our school to get his training and registration papers."

To make our talks more graphic, we decided to shoot a

movie to illustrate our work. On film we showed trainers who purposely tripped and stumbled when the dogs made mistakes. The men feigned clumsiness and ran into things over and over again until the trainee's common sense took over and the "Phooey!" the guide dogs detested so much was replaced by an unvarying "That's a good girl!"

In one reel was a sequence in which I walked a block with Buddy—a block that contained two awnings, the near one high, the far low. We started off at a brisk pace and passed freely under the first. As we approached the second, viewers could see that if I proceeded to clip along, it would hit me across the eyes. Buddy, without even seeming to look up, neatly swung around it, avoiding it smoothly and completely. Her beautifully executed bit of work made such an impression that most audiences burst into spontaneous tribute to her skill.

I will never forget a visit to Washington, D.C., about this time. I was scheduled to make a talk and show our film before a large group that included Mr. Cordell Hull, then my home state's most distinguished citizen. I wanted everything to go especially smoothly. I was, as usual, to operate the motion picture projector, and I rechecked the sprocket clamp and take-up reels and spindles until—pardon the expression—I could have done it with my eyes shut.

Our procedure was to set up the machine in the center aisle of the hall where we were to perform, from which position I would make a few introductory remarks. Then, as much to illustrate Buddy's guiding ability as to place me in a more advantageous position for speaking, she would take me down the center aisle to the platform for my talk. When, during it, I was ready to use the projector, Buddy would return me to it by the same route we had used to reach the stage.

On this occasion, in order to test Buddy's efficiency at leading me in and out of a maze of trouble, the people in charge, without informing me, quietly blocked our return with chairs.

86

Not only that, they suspended a barrier that might strike my
head, and literally strewed even the floor of the center aisle
with obstacles.

When I picked up the harness to leave the stage, I stopped
at the foot of the steps and gave the proper command, "Right!"
To my surprise and consternation, Buddy refused to obey me
The audience was absolutely hushed. I had no idea what was
wrong, but I trusted my dog. I gave her her head. She had
watched the whole proceedings from the platform and had
seen the complicated series of impediments set up for us. Without a second's hesitation she simply took me the quickest,
safest way to our destination. She led me up the *outer* aisle,
across the back of the auditorium, and down the rear of the
center aisle to the projector.

The audience went wild with applause. Buddy had given a
far more remarkable demonstration of her prowess than they
had anticipated. Instead of attempting to run the chaotic
obstacle course, she had taken the common-sense way out of
our predicament. "Whew!" an admirer told us afterward, "that
girl's really got initiative!" Another marveled, "She's not only
trained, she's *educated!*"

Buddy's appearances and the film were so successful that
far-sighted Mrs. Eustis suggested that we make a speaking
tour of a number of schools, both public and private.

"There you'll reach the youngsters who will grow up to be
the leaders in their communities—the ones who will be in the
most opportune position to help us in our work and to help all
those who are handicapped," she said.

How right she was in her judgment has been proven many
times. Eventually many of our most active volunteer workers
were boys and girls who first became interested in Seeing Eye
through our initial meeting at the school talks.

We followed the "Three-R" circuit from Maine to Illinois,
down through Virginia and the Carolinas. Buddy enjoyed the

young people. She barked approvingly at their applause and enjoyed their adulation when our talks were over. She loved to stand and have them pet her, one by one. She did not even object when some of the more enthusiastic plucked hairs from her coat as souvenirs.

Buddy and I were such a good team that in some places they just would not believe I was really blind. One appearance at a military school almost turned out to be a rout when the future officers decided to indulge in a little "humor in uniform." During my talk, with Buddy at my feet, I could feel that she was holding her head in a taut kind of way. Every so often she would move it alertly from side to side, as if keeping a wary eye out for trouble. Simultaneously I heard the boys in the front row trying unsuccessfully to suppress giggles.

I surmised that they had smuggled in a cat and were showing it to Buddy. Taking a chance that our guess was correct, I simply stopped speaking, then pointed in the direction where I had left the headmaster, and said, "Sir, will you please put the cat in the back of the room?"

Afterwards I stayed for lunch, and the cadets kept coming to our table and passing their hands back and forth across my face, because they would not believe that I could not see.

Their incredulity did not spoil my appetite, nor Buddy's. She behaved shamelessly.

As we rose to leave, the youngsters all politely stood. Every curious eye was directly upon us. Near the exit we passed a tray of apple pies cooling on a rack for that night's supper. Buddy just brazenly snatched one, made it disappear like a canine Houdini, and kept right on going. The kids hooted with delight.

As you can see, some of our successes were purely accidental—and we were lucky that they did not end up as pure accidents. At one school, after setting up the projector, I gave Buddy the command "Forward," as usual, to go down the aisle and up on the platform. We approached a ramp which bridged the orchestra pit at the left side aisle of the auditorium and then crossed to center stage.

After my talk we returned by the same route. That is, I *thought* it was the same. Actually, while we talked, the boys had prankishly rolled away the movable ramp and substituted a narrow catwalk over the pit. We had negotiated a precarious bridge that would have made a sighted person tremble. Had I realized what we were attempting, I would not have tried it without a safety belt and a net!

At some of these schools I was not too much older than the seniors. At one very select academy for young ladies I let my desire to impress them run away with me and bragged that I had been quite a horseman before my loss of sight.

"I've even had several good canters with my old favorite mount since," I declared recklessly.

"Splendid," they cried. "Ride with us this afternoon!"

As we trotted off, the girls neglected to tell me that their horses were jumpers. I soon thought mine was a flyer. Unlike Buddy, my unknown Pegasus gave me no notice whatsoever of the obstacles in our path or that he intended to soar over every one. Each time he unexpectedly leapt through space, my heart kept pace and leapt to my mouth. You can imagine my relief at getting back to the stables sound of limb.

Two good things came of the experience: I never boasted again of my riding ability, and I have never since been foolish enough to trust myself to any four-legged animal except Buddy.

At Bennington College the president thoughtfully suggested that I let Buddy loose for a romp over their beautiful campus. She soon came dashing back, smelling of a most peculiar odor. "Polecat!" cried the girls. Apparently the kitty had let Buddy have it right in the face, for in hysterical agitation she rubbed her head against my trouser leg, then ran among the flustered girls, trying to get rid of the odor by brushing against their clothing, too.

Next morning the campus dormitories looked more like laundries. Dresses, skirts, stockings, and jackets hung out of windows for airing. I also understand that we caused the prexy to make an unanticipated change of headquarters after Buddy and I spent the night in his suite. We left Bennington under rather an unfragrant cloud. My attitude, of course, was that it was not my dog that had caused the trouble, but their cat.

I took Buddy to a veterinarian in Albany and paid ten dollars to have her deodorized, but no one performed the same service for me. For about a month, whenever I went into a hotel room on a damp day, the bellboy would sniff and say, "I'd better phone down and get a different room; this one has an odd odor." Knowing the futility of his finding one—with me along—that did not have it, I always said, "What a clean smell! I think I rather like it. Don't bother the desk, we'll be quite comfortable here!"

Buddy's relationships with other animals did not always have such spectacular or lingering consequences, but they were often notable. At a state convention of a service club in Ohio, in response to a question, I made the flat statement, "No, Buddy never fights. Seeing Eye dogs mind their own business."

A few minutes later we went outside to give a demonstration, and a little fox terrier ran up and joined us, yapping and snapping at Buddy's heels. True to her training, Buddy paid no attention at all to it, concentrating on the commands and executing every one perfectly. As we wheeled to make a return to our starting point, the spitfire came in again, intending presumably to nip and worry all the way back. Buddy, without slowing down or neglecting her duties, just reached over and took a piece out of the terrier. Its yap became a yelp and the heckler ran off, her tail between her legs.

"Thought you said Buddy never fought," someone observed, laughing.

"I wouldn't call that a fight, would you?" I replied. But after that I always answered queries with "Buddy *seldom* fights."

This was certainly true. She had only five battles in all the years I had her, and two of these were with the same dog. She never started a tussle, but when she was forced into one, she did not leap around and bark and make a lot of nervous noise like most dogs. She just stood solidly on her four feet and let her attacker come within distance. Then she went right for the throat. When it was all over, her adversary needed a veterinarian.

Buddy was never jealous of other dogs, even if I petted and played with them, for she knew that I loved her and no other. If I picked up a little dog, she would join us as if to say, "Hello there! How is everything in the world of you small ones?"

Quite often, if a tiny Peke or poodle in an elevator growled or even snapped at her, she would just raise up on her back feet and look at it. If she got a chance, she would reach over and give it a lick, one that would say, "Oh, come now! Use some sense. You know if I wanted to, I could swallow you in one mouthful."

A friend of mine in Nashville was given a little fox terrier his family would not let him keep, so he brought it over to us. Buddy immediately made herself the little fellow's guardian and took excellent care of him. If he cried at night, she would go get him and all three of us would sleep together. Even after the puppy was fully grown, my dog was his "Buddy" in the warmest sense of the word.

On one train trip, even though the public was widely accepting guide dogs, Buddy had to ride again in the baggage car. I was concerned about it and went back the first thing in the morning to ask if she was all right.

"You needn't have worried," said the baggage man. "She had company. A forlorn little bulldog puppy taking its first ride was whimpering and trembling enough to break your heart. I could see Buddy wasn't going to let that go on long. She reached over and pulled it to her and mothered it. That contented little pup slept between her paws all night. Both of them got along fine!"

Buddy's tender nature was such that she did not seem to know that felines were supposed to be her species' traditional enemies. She and The Seeing Eye cat were pals. When we got back to the office after one jaunt, her friend had some new kittens. Buddy, who had been investigating to see what was new during our absence, found them. Carefully picking one of them up, she brought it in to me, as if telling me, "Look what's happened while we were away." She was as proud as if she had been responsible for the litter herself.

Chapter 8

BUDDY loved our trips. When I was getting ready to go, she would stand and watch me pack. If I put her curry comb and brush in first, she would contentedly wait, but if I arranged everything else before including them, she would pace around me, then press against my knees, as if saying, "Be sure you squeeze in my things, too."

She was immensely fond of traveling by car. Although she liked the boys who drove me, she treated them with cool detachment. "You're here to do certain things for us," was her attitude. "That's all, and as far as we go." She would reach over in the morning from the back seat, which was hers, give them a lick behind the ear and sit up straight as if she had just said, "Let's get going."

She arranged herself in a position of extreme elegance, one front paw draped over the arm rest, with a genteel bend at the wrist, and her bright eyes at just the right level to look out of the window with no effort on her part. Not only did she take keen interest in everything we passed but she expected others, except me, who had a good excuse, to do likewise. This was clearly demonstrated when a young lady riding in the back seat with her closed her eyes and leaned back to relax after a long Seeing Eye meeting. After looking at her dozing companion disapprovingly for a few minutes, Buddy took careful aim with her wet nose and knocked her hat off. It was just a hint that people who have precious eyes should take advantage of the big, bright, wonderful world about us.

Most of our automobile trips were fun for us both, but one turned out to be a nightmare of an experience. Speeding down a Pennsylvania road one day, our driver misjudged a curve and shot off into the soft shoulder that lined the highway. The desperate yank he gave the steering wheel to get us back on the road sent us spinning, and we turned over three times.

With difficulty we opened the car doors. The driver was not hurt at all. I felt some stinging pain in my forehead but thought of nothing but Buddy, who was lying outside on the grass, whimpering. She was cut badly. Her paws were bleeding and her nose was cut.

The emergency lent us strength, and after a struggle we got the car back on its wheels and rushed as fast as we dared on to Pittsburgh. I ran into the hotel, took a room, and quickly called over two veterinarians. While they worked over Buddy, I was on the phone to Morristown, reporting the accident, when a man came in and said, "I am Dr. Jones."

"Fine," I said, motioning him to the couch. "Buddy's over there."

"Oh, no," he said, "I've come to look at you."

It was the first time I realized that my face and arms and chest were bleeding, for the windshield glass had cut clean through my overcoat and sweater. I had been so concerned for my seeing eyes that I had forgotten the rest of me.

Buddy and I spent some time recuperating. We were pronounced "completely mended" on the same day, as if it were fated that one's progress would keep pace with the other so that we could resume our travels in tandem.

On our talking trips I learned something from Buddy every day. She showed special sympathy for anyone who was handicapped in any way. If a blind person or someone with a crutch sat on the aisle as we proceeded to the lecture platform, she would stop and give him a friendly lick. On the street she would pull me several feet out of our way if necessary to greet a spastic in a wheel chair or to thrust a sociable nose at a maimed beggar sitting on the sidewalk.

Once she gave particular notice to a person who my driver said apparently had nothing wrong with him. Minutes later the man she had saluted told me, "I was touched by your dog's understanding attention. She seemed to know that a few weeks ago I suffered a severe heart attack."

Buddy's compassion seemed unlimited at the first school for the blind that we visited. She stood like a statue while each of the 203 children ran a chubby hand from the tip of her nose to the tip of her tail. They felt the U-shaped harness, which made the difference between having an ordinary dog and one that meant eyes to you. Every now and then she would nuzzle a little child, as if to say, "Someday you will be free. One of my coworkers will be your eyes, and you will glory in being your own master."

Buddy was uncannily sensitive to the nature of people. Both Billy Debetaz and Jack Humphrey, who handled hundreds of dogs, recognized her peculiar gift. Her character readings were so penetrating that I came to accept them almost without question. One evening in Kansas City a man called up from the lobby of our hotel and asked to see me. I invited him up, but when he appeared in the doorway, Buddy growled at him. I silenced her and the visitor started to come in. Quick as a flash Buddy threw herself across his feet, forbidding him to enter. Trusting her, I said, "Perhaps we had better talk here in the doorway."

He seemed to me a pleasant kind of person, and I leaned against the jamb and listened with interest to his proposal to raise money for Seeing Eye through charity bazaars. Later I found that Buddy's first impression proved truer than mine.

The hotel manager told me that my caller was a notorious crook. His specialty was setting up gambling parties in the name of a charity and then making off with the proceeds.

She seemed to be able to tell the difference between a person who was deliberately doing something wrong and one who got himself into trouble without meaning to. On a streetcar in Allentown, Pennsylvania, just as we were going round a curve, a man reaching up to take a package from the overhead rack lost his balance and fell heavily on top of her.

"Oof!" grunted Buddy, then rolled herself clear. She whirled to face her attacker and bared her teeth menacingly.

"I didn't mean to do it! Don't let her bite me!" cried the poor man in terror. He threw his arms protectingly around his head and lay still, apparently expecting to be torn limb from limb. But Buddy, although the wind had been pretty well knocked out of her, seemed to understand that it had been an accident, and merely ran a forgiving tongue over his face.

Even when it came to women—that very complicated sex— Buddy did not need a crystal ball to divine character. Nor did she need a sample of my date's handwriting to predict whether she was a playgirl who liked the bright lights and the crowds or a homebody who thought two was perfect company.

Buddy was so good at this type of fortune telling that I came to look to her for pointers as to the kind of evening a date would prefer. If, when a lady friend and I stopped by my room for a cocktail, Buddy took her usual place on my bed, I assumed that she could tell that the girl wanted to spend the evening on the town. Occasionally, however, Buddy would forsake her customary resting place and recline on the sofa or in a chair. That meant a cozy evening at home was on the agenda.

Following Buddy's clues often put me on the right track immediately. I seldom found her judgment in error.

Judgment was really Buddy's long suit. Two different experiences with separate desperadoes showed that she invariably knew when to open her mouth and when to keep it closed—which is a better record than I can claim for her master.

One sultry summer night when I stopped over in Nashville en route to a speaking engagement, my mother made up a bed for Buddy and me on our screened-in sleeping porch. In the middle of the night I awoke with an odd feeling to find that Buddy was not in her usual place beside me. Then an ominous sound broke the night silence—the rasping noise of someone carefully cutting the screen in an attempt to reach the fastening. More silence. Then a piercing yell, a combination of fright and pain, rent the air, followed by the racket of running footsteps.

Buddy then calmly came back to bed. Apparently she had heard the housebreaker before I had, quietly padded over to the window, and stood by. When the ruffian cautiously put his hand through, feeling for the latch, he found instead a set of good sharp, businesslike teeth.

Buddy might have handled the situation differently—she probably could have frightened the burglar away sooner with a bark, but the silent treatment strategy that she decided upon added an element of terror to the surprise. I doubted, after the lesson she gave him—complete with souvenir tooth marks for emphasis, that he would soon return to a house so specially guarded. The next morning Buddy accepted everyone's praise as if to say, "It's all in the day's or night's work!"

That was the time Buddy opened her mouth. Another time, in Detroit, she showed her good sense by doing the opposite. It was dusk, and I had taken her to an alley behind the Book Cadillac Hotel to give her a chance to powder her nose. Suddenly a thief came up behind me and stuck a pistol in my back. "Hand over your money and watch," he ordered.

I was terrified that Buddy would attack him and be shot. But she simply came to my side and stood quite still. She had seen revolvers in Switzerland, where she had watched police dogs being trained, and doubtless remembered that guns can do a lot of harm.

I handed my timepiece and wallet over my shoulder to him and said, "The watch won't do you any good, but it means a lot to me. It's specially made for the blind."

"Cripes," he exclaimed. "I ain't robbin' a blind guy!" and handed back both items as if they had burned his fingers.

A week or so afterward I was asked to speak to the boys in a state reformatory. It happened that one lad asked me if I ever felt afraid, traveling around the country, unable to see if anyone tried to take advantage of me. "I'd think you'd be duck soup for some dip or hold-up artist," he commented.

In answer I told about my recent experience in the Michigan alley.

"That robber wasn't such a bad egg, after all," observed one teen-ager.

"Don't be a dope!" exclaimed another. "Any stupe knows it's bad luck to steal from a blind man!"

A man could not have had a better traveling companion than Buddy. She showed her intelligence in all kinds of situations. As we came off the train at Pennsylvania Station in New York once, the Pullman attendant summoned a redcap who picked up our two pieces of luggage, and we proceeded down the platform. We had not gone far when Buddy stopped and refused to go any farther.

"She's lookin' at the bags, suh," the porter spoke up. "She's eyein' 'em mighty peculiar."

Buddy then turned me around and led us back to our car. There the conductor was trying to pacify an irate man who was insisting, "But that is not my bag!" We exchanged a suitcase with him and everybody was happy, particularly

Buddy. She cavorted all around in little leaps, furiously wagging her tail and accepting all the praise heaped on her as if she knew how richly she deserved it.

Although on our trips I usually took Buddy out myself for her play and exercise, I let a bellboy take over for me once in Atlantic City. The spray was high on the boardwalk, and Buddy looked forward to a brisk outing. Instead of that, the bellboy decided that this was a good time to show off "a trick dog" to his friends and gathered a group for Buddy to amuse. Bored with purposeless "fetching" and other aimless commands, she slipped her collar and ran away from the young impresario.

Worried almost sick when he could not find her, he came up to my room to confess what had happened. I never heard such relief in a person's voice as when he saw Buddy lying in the corner. She had been home for some three quarters of an hour, having come straight to the hotel and stepped on the elevator. The operator, who knew her, let her off at the fifth floor, and in a few seconds she was scratching at our door. She regarded the bellboy with a stare as if to say, "I guess that will teach you! If a lady's escort expects too much of her, there's only one thing for her to do—get out of his clutches and walk home!"

As our travel miles piled up, I found few situations that could cause me worry. I had so much confidence in Buddy that my attitude came to be, "Bring on the problems, my dog'll handle them!" In every crisis she summed up each situation and took action appropriate to the occasion.

One night in Philadelphia I stopped at the reception desk to chat with the clerk. A guest complained loudly to him for letting me interrupt his service. "I'm sorry," I said, and walked on into the drugstore.

The stranger followed me and started bawling me out. Then he gave me a shove. I was surprised that Buddy did not tear him to pieces. Instead, she raised herself calmly and quietly on her back legs and gave my assailant a firm but gentle push. He landed on the floor, his anger lost in his surprise. Then Buddy quickly stepped into position in front of me, as if to say, "Let's get out of here." I picked up the harness, she stepped us quickly to the elevator, and we went back to our room.

Next morning when we descended for breakfast, the manager stopped me at the elevator and said, "Please, sir, don't come into the lobby just now. The man who bothered you last night is here. He has escaped from an asylum and his family are coming for him."

Once again I was grateful for Buddy's intuition. She had sensed my attacker's abnormality and acted accordingly. And I was not the only one who was grateful. The night before, the manager had had visions of violence in the lobby followed by ruinous damage suits. Instead, Buddy had acted so sensibly that she had avoided both catastrophes. He was so thankful that he could not do enough for her.

It happened that a noisy convention was in progress at the hotel at the time and we were not getting much sleep because of four obstreperous neighbors. One of these drunks telephoned the desk and complained about being in a room next to a dog. "Ish this an animal shelter?" he demanded. "Lisshen, we or the dog musht go!"

The manager agreed wholeheartedly, put down the phone, went upstairs with a staff of brawny Irish bouncers who promptly threw the quartet onto the street!

That was not the only occasion when Buddy's good behavior turned a hotel into "a home away from home." One cold morning in Philadelphia I was awakened by Buddy licking my face, telling me she urgently wanted to go out. It was very early and I was surprised at her impatience. I dragged myself out of bed and pulled on my clothes. I will not put down here the things I said under my breath about that dog. As I opened the door to the closet to get my coat, I was met with a rush of hot, suffocating smoke.

Coughing all the time, I telephoned downstairs, told them the closet was on fire, put the harness and leash on Buddy, and we caught the elevator to the lobby. The linen cupboard on the floor below us was in flames. Fortunately Buddy gave the alarm in time to prevent their spreading farther. She was a popular dog around those diggings, not only then, but every time we returned

On our circuit Buddy soon became better known than her master. I went into many hotels where we had been before and heard the clerk say, "Why, Buddy, we're so glad to have you back again!" And then, to me, "I beg your pardon, sir. Will you please give me your name? We must have it to register you."

One time in Pittsburgh when I arrived about one o'clock on a Saturday afternoon to change trains for Morristown, I found myself without any money. After going to about four hotels and trying unsuccessfully to get a check cashed, we came to one where the dog was remembered, though I was not. As we headed for the cashier's window, a bellboy called, "Hey, Buddy!" She turned around and licked his hand. That was my identification, and my signature was honored.

Frequently during our travels I was the target of religious fanatics. As I was finishing my breakfast coffee at the Statler Hotel in Boston one morning, a man came over to my table and sat himself down without even asking my permission. He immediately launched into a long harangue about the miracles of faith healing.

When he gave me a chance to break in, I stood up to leave and told him it had all been very inspiring. He grasped my sleeve and said he wanted to come up to my room and read the Bible to me.

I tried to be polite, for I respect anyone's religious feelings, but he became so insistent that I finally said, "I appreciate your interest, but my sight cannot be restored, because I do not have my natural eyes any more. These are artificial."

"If you believe properly," he said wildly, "God will grow you a new pair of eyes."

I had had about all I could stand of his accusations of my lack of faith. At the risk of sounding blasphemous, I broke his zealous hold on my arm and said, "If He does, I'll be grateful, but I'll also be out of a job!"

Shortly after this unnerving brush with forcible conversion I gave seven talks in one day in Pittsburgh and returned to my hotel room after ten o'clock at night, completely exhausted. As I undressed, I heard a knock on the door and a voice said, "I am Reverend Hugh Clark of the Calvary Episcopal Church."

"Another fanatic," I said under my breath, and, aloud, "Brother, if you want to read the Bible to somebody, go down into the lobby and hire a bellboy to listen. I revere God's word, but tonight I'm just too tired for ecclesiastics.

"However," I added, opening the door slightly, "if you will have a drink with me, come on in."

The Reverend laughed good-humoredly. "I'll be happy to," he said. He proved to be one of the most stimulating and delightful people I ever met. Over a rejuvenating Scotch and soda we talked about God, life, and man until five in the morning and have been close friends ever since.

One snowy winter night we were staying on the twentieth floor of the Palmer House in Chicago. Because people had fed her things she should not have eaten so late at night, Buddy received a hurry call. I had to get up, dress myself, and go with her through several winding corridors to the elevator. At that time of night the lift did not descend to street level, so we had to get off at the main lobby. Buddy took me down the stairs, through the arcade, and into the alley, where it was sleeting.

Shivering as I waited, I angrily resented having to go to all this trouble. Buddy, with her sensitivity, felt my impatience.

Then, all of a sudden, a chastening thought struck me. If I, alone, had had to come out into the night on an errand, I could not have made it without Buddy. I felt ashamed of myself for my irritability. What about all the times Buddy had eagerly, without a trace of even mild resistance, taken me where I wanted to go? Maybe she would much rather have spent her days roaming in a field instead of patiently sitting quietly in auditoriums. But never by so much as the tiniest peevish bark did she ever indicate that leading my life—as she did in the fullest sense of the expression—was not her ideal of the way to spend hers. She seemed happiest when she was in harness and we were together as two halves that complemented each other to make a complete entity.

The night did not seem so cold now. I reached down and gave Buddy a good pat and a happy hug. She responded immediately, her forgiving nature blotting out all remembrance of my petulance. We went back upstairs again, a man who was wiser and a dog that was happier. Buddy crawled up on the foot of the bed and we both went to sleep, I'm afraid, with a little moistness in our eyes—the dog that had been reassured that her master loved and needed her and the man grateful for the contentment and independence she had brought him.

The wonderful blossoming of our students was immensely rewarding to us. If our pleasure in their progress could have been turned into legal tender, we would have had no difficulty in paying the butcher, the baker, and the harness-handle maker.

Our expenses were increasing by leaps and bounds—and I do not confine the expression to the activities of the kennels—

as we enrolled more and more students. We needed money to carry out remodeling plans and to enlarge our staff. Mrs. Eustis had enlisted the financial aid of a few of her close friends, but she and they could not keep up with the demands occasioned by our rapid expansion.

That is the reason why Buddy and I began to move in the circles of high society. Our "debut" was all in a good cause.

To enlarge our group of sponsors, Mrs. Eustis arranged for us to be invited along with her for weekends in the homes of her wealthy and fashionable friends. The host would ask a group in to see our movie and hear the story of Seeing Eye. Buddy and I were "Exhibit A," the end product of the organization. These new friends could be helpful, not only in a monetary way and in giving jobs to our blind in factories but in arranging to open the streetcars, busses, and hotels to our guides.

The tea-party teaspoon became a silver springboard by which we hurdled many barriers that normally would have been surmounted only by months of slow, painstaking work.

In New Haven, for example, we visited with a lovely couple named Otterson, who became very interested in Buddy and our work. We were eager to open hotels in Connecticut to the guide dogs. So the Ottersons arranged a party and invited, among other guests, a director of a large bank which had controlling interest in a chain of hotels that dotted the state.

The banker showed keen interest and kindly invited Mrs. Otterson to bring Buddy and me to tea. Over little lemon cakes we continued unhurried talk about Morristown, our host continually punctuating the conversation with, "How beautifully your dog behaves!"

As we said our good-bys, Mrs. Otterson inquired, "Of course, Albert, you will direct your hotels to admit these wonderful dogs?"

"Certainly," he replied amiably. "I had no other thought."

I almost stumbled right there in the smooth hallway. Having already attempted to get the same permission through a straight business call and been refused even contact with any official, I could not help but think, "The answer you get often depends on who asks the question."

I remember visiting the estate of Reginald Auchincloss in Tuxedo Park. We had a wonderful time. Buddy was very adept at taking me around the new surroundings, moving easily from, say, the formal gardens to the croquet lawn. We even went out on a well-stocked private lake, our little craft propelled by an electric motor—to avoid poisoning the fish.

As a matter of fact, Buddy was so well "my eyes" that her skill almost lost us a sponsor. A well-to-do industrialist came to Mrs. Eustis and said, "I'm ashamed to say I thought your Mr. Frank was a faker. He and that dog get along so well I just couldn't believe he was blind.

"I even laid a bet against myself that he wasn't," he continued. "I had to sidle right up next to him at luncheon to convince myself he wasn't putting on an act."

The guest then handed the Boss a generous check. "Here's the wager I lost. I'm glad to contribute, after what I've seen today. I think you're working miracles at Morristown!"

Buddy saw to it that she herself never sank in the social swim. Her wants were few, but she did have a growing girl's appetite. Her manner of satisfying it was always somehow appropriate to the situation. At home alone with me, she would never filch a thing. She was too honorable—or, perhaps like the boy at the reform school, she knew it was bad luck to steal from the blind. I could lay out food or cocktail tidbits and she would never touch them. But when company came— sighted and therefore able to look out for themselves—no holds were barred.

At our fashionable friends' palatial homes she carried on her peculations under a cover of immense dignity. Once at an elegant tea party in Boston, amid a buzz of polite conversation, the butler served sandwiches from a tea cart. When it rolled up to me, its lower tray was right on a level with Buddy's nose. Though her head did not move nor an eye flicker, in less time than it takes to tell it, a stack of sandwiches disappeared. Only one person, Mrs. Eustis, who happened to have her eyes directly on Buddy at the moment, saw the snatch. It was, Mrs. Eustis said, as if a dowager, in a moment when she thought herself unobserved, without even so much as lowering her lorgnette, surreptitiously put out a well-shod foot and scraped a fallen wallet under her skirt.

Buddy and I once asked for an appointment with the president of a big insurance company to ask him for a contribution. He welcomed us, gave me an armchair, then sat down again at his desk. I told him all about our work and how his money could help. He was most attentive and gave me a much-appreciated check. As I thanked him and rose to leave, I heard Buddy's feet hit the floor as she got down from some piece of furniture to my right. I reached over and found that she had been making herself comfortable on a luxuriously upholstered *chaise longue.*

When I started giving her a severe scolding, the donor said, "Oh, no. Don't say a word to her. All the time you were talking, she had her head on the back of the chaise, gazing straight at me. It wasn't what you said that made me give you the thousand dollars; it was looking into that dog's eyes. I just couldn't refuse her."

My contacts with the affluent sometimes took me into water out of my depth. Occasionally, we were invited to the horse races. Buddy loved the excitement. From the "They're off!" shout, she stood stock still, her nose "pointing" the furious action around the oval. She participated as much as if she herself had shoved the money over the counter for our two-dollar tickets. Every few seconds she gave one sharp whisk of her tail and a quick snort, as if to say, "Our horse is still in there, but, brother, you never know!"

My custom was to take twenty-five dollars to the track and no more. If I lost, I philosophically considered that the cost of the afternoon's entertainment. But one day I went with a quartet of sportsmen whose own colors were racing that day. Sitting there in their box, just as big as if I, too, had my own stables, went to my head. I recklessly took their advice and that of other wealthy track habitues who, loaded with "dope sheets," had just come back from the paddocks. Each one had it "straight from the horse's mouth" and kindly let me in on the names of "surefire winners."

As a result of their thoughtfulness, at the end of the sixth race I had dropped one hundred and twenty-five dollars. That was just one hundred dollars more than I could afford to lose.

In the seventh race was an entry named Blind Barney. In the eighth was another, called Black Buddy. Nobody but their own jockeys had ever heard of them. For obvious reasons, I bet on them. These beautiful long shots not only made up my losses. I came away from the track some two hundred dollars richer.

I will not reveal what those fashionable people called themselves and their paddock pals—experts who could not see a winner as well as a blind man.

So, as you can see, it was not all work and no play. Buddy and I between "prospecting trips," as I called our fund-seeking excursions, and speaking tours, managed to get back to Morristown for at least part of every month. There Buddy, the veteran, enjoyed brass-hatting it over the other dogs who were mere rookies still in basic training.

She disdained the company of the neophytes. If we started down the street in a group of blind students and their dogs, she would either stall and hold me far in the rear or increase her pace until she passed the others and headed the procession herself. She was not going to be mistaken for just another guide dog. *She* was Buddy, the first and most special of all!

It is a pleasant fact that any Seeing Eye graduate will tell you quite sincerely that his is the very smartest and most beautiful dog ever turned out by the school. Mine really was. She enjoyed showing how superior she was to all the rest. When I dropped a glove or box of matches, she would pick it up and return it and look around with a complacent air which amused onlookers. She seemed to be saying, "It isn't necessary to applaud, but how's that for technique?"

As we were just half a dozen miles from Openaka, we went back for a weekend with the Ebelings as often as we could. Buddy adored these holidays. There was the lake to swim in, a flower bed that was a grand place to bury bones—dogs came before roses at Openaka—and our own room with a large double bed that held us both comfortably.

A spacious, much-mended counterpane, known as "Buddy's spread," was always hauled out and put on this bed during our visits—a necessary precaution, for after a swim in the lake she enjoyed dashing upstairs and onto the bed to dry herself. I'll never forget how, during the days when Openaka was our makeshift Seeing Eye headquarters, she loved to lie on that spread and look out the window at the current class of student dogs being put through their exercises in the big run in front of the kennel.

She took everything in so completely that I expected her, with the wisdom of an old grad, to give me a detailed report on the pupils: "That blonde Suzie isn't heeling correctly." Or, "Tom II did well when he was put on long leash today!"

Actually we both loved that bed. I did a lot of listening to the radio in it. I have always been a horror-story fan and can remember the dreadful times when those thrillers caught up with me as a boy, and caused chilling nightmares. I would

yell out, "Save me!" and, "Help! Help!" in the middle
of the night. I would moan and groan and suffer a seemingly
interminable time until some member of the family heard me
and rescued me.

But these days, at my first murmur, Buddy would reach up,
give me a reassuring nudge and a comforting lick. I never
really suffered from a nightmare after she started sleeping
with me. I could listen to a whole series of radio whodunits;
my own "private eye" protected me from night fears.

On one of our visits with the Ebelings Buddy gave another
clear demonstration that she was a thinking being. A new
flight of stairs to the second floor was under construction. The
treads were finished, but the railing was not up. I anticipated
no trouble, however, because the passageway was wide. By
keeping my shoulder close to the wall as I went to and from
our room, I should have no difficulty.

Buddy was never expected to do anything for me when she
was not in harness; she was free to romp and play, forget her
duties. But the first time I started up that uncompleted stair-
case, she dashed to my side. She could see that the protecting
barrier was missing, so she provided my safeguard. Up she
went with me, step by step, keeping herself between me and
the open ends of the treads. During our entire stay she never
let me out of her sight, rushing to escort me each time I went
up or down, pressing me against the wall, forcing me away
from the hazardous brink. She spent very little time out of
doors that weekend; she was too busy being a perambulating
banister.

One raw, rainy day on one of our other visits Buddy
scratched on the kitchen door, and Mrs. Ebeling let her in.

"Shall I put her on leash until supper is ready?" I asked.

"I don't think you need to," she answered. "Everything is
on the stove cooking. I don't think she'd touch anything there,
do you?"

"She never has," I replied. And we went on to continue our conversation in the living room.

Going into the kitchen a few minutes later to make sure that the meal was coming along properly, Mrs. Ebeling found Buddy on her hind legs, her front paws resting on the window sill. She was gazing earnestly out the back window at the ice house, a building which she had seen hundreds of times and in which she had never before shown the slightest interest.

On the floor lay an empty saucepan which had contained melted butter for the asparagus. A small yellow trickle showed at the side of Buddy's mouth. The story of how she had managed to remove the heated saucepan from the top of the electric stove, with several rings red hot, without burning herself and without making any noise, is still referred to as "The Great Openaka Range Robbery."

Buddy loved to swim, and one Sunday I took her—or she took me—to the lake with a girl friend of mine. This was at a time when rubber bathing suits were fashionable, and my date was wearing *le dernier cri*.

Buddy had a habit of paddling from one swimmer to another, greeting them by putting her forepaws up on their shoulders. She did this to my girl, who, not expecting the attention, pulled away in a hurry. As she jerked back, Buddy's paws traveled down the front of her suit. They slit that Goodyear creation as cleanly and swiftly as if her nails had been as many razor blades.

Buddy and I had to go clear back to the house to get her a towel so she could leave the water in modesty. I felt it was very unfair, my being blind and therefore unable to enjoy the situation to its fullest!

Buddy particularly relished swimming to an old log raft anchored in the middle of the lake. She would climb on it and bask in the sun. As time went on, the raft grew more and more water-logged until it would bear the weight of only one, or at most two light persons. Then it was Buddy's delight to swim out and climb quietly aboard so that it would submerge and give her friends a ducking.

Once I started to swim out to the raft but missed it. In the course of circling around trying to locate it, I lost all sense of direction. I had been struggling quite a while before I began to give up hope of finding it. Suddenly I realized with some panic that I was fast becoming exhausted.

I wanted to return to shore, but did not know which way to head. For all I knew, I might be striking out for the far side of the lake. As usual when I needed help, I thought of Buddy. I called for her, hoping she would not be out of range of the sound of my voice. She gave the most welcome answering bark I ever heard to let me know she was on the way. She hit the water with a resounding splash and in a few minutes was by my side.

I reached for her collar and almost before I could say, "That's a *good* girl!" she had led me back to the beach and safety.

The fight to make the guide dog acceptable in public places was not easily won. Increasing numbers of our graduates who were well on the way to becoming earners and useful members of society instead of liabilities were drastically hampered by the discrimination against their dogs in all sorts of basic territories from restaurants to railway cars.

Mrs. Eustis and I fought it out on these fronts together and at all opportunities. Driving up through Connecticut once, we stopped at a very nice inn for lunch.

"Morris, I'll go ahead and get a table," she said. "I'll bet you a new hat it will take you more than ten minutes to join me with Buddy."

After giving her time to be seated, Buddy and I went in.

"I'm sorry, sir," the headwaiter began, "but——."

"Buddy, forward!" I commanded.

She did as I expected—went straight to Mrs. Eustis, who was quite surprised that we had come so far so soon.

The headwaiter was right with us, but we had occupied the disputed territory. Possession is nine points of the law, and we were not going to be routed. I explained just loud enough to be heard at least ten tables away how wonderful it was to have a dog to be your eyes. He again started with, "I am sorry, sir," but I cut right in with, "It's wonderful how well Buddy behaves—" and here I raised my voice even a little more, "—it is so embarrassing when I have to argue about bringing her with me."

"Sir, I am sorry," the harassed man once more tried to protest, but I steam-rollered on with, "—because that calls attention to the fact that I have to have a dog!"

By that time the other luncheon guests were shooting looks fit to kill at the headwaiter, who slunk away toward the kitchen. We never found out if his vocabulary went any farther than the four words he had been able to get out with such difficulty.

Mrs. Eustis was delighted at our strategy. She was a person of magnificent verve, with a good sense of humor and a hearty laugh, and if you were right, she was with you 500 per cent. We used this system, her running interference for Buddy and me, with considerable success for several years. All we needed, actually, was enough time in a place for Buddy to show how well behaved she could be. Invariably she gave the major-domos of countless dining rooms a good lesson in Seeing Eye dog conduct and they were usually glad after that to welcome guide dogs as guests.

"The Boss," as I called Mrs. Eustis, and I were in New York to have lunch with John D. Rockefeller, Jr.; we were eager to part some of his money from him for the benefit of The Seeing Eye. We arrived several minutes early at the

Élysée for our engagement. The hotel manager, elegant in black coat and morning trousers, was adamant against admitting Buddy to the dining room, so I "checked" her in the cloakroom which flanked the dining-area entrance. She obeyed my commands "Down" and "Rest" beautifully.

Mrs. Eustis and I carefully chose a corner table, not too far from the door, and Mr. Rockefeller appeared a few minutes later. When the greetings were over, I told him, "You must meet an important member of our organization." I whistled low, and Buddy came very quietly in, said hello, and with no commotion at all lay down under the table.

Old Striped Pants paced up and down, but he dared not offend so exalted a patron as Mr. Rockefeller. When we left, he was so relieved that Buddy had caused no trouble that he unbent completely, praised and patted her and said cordially, "Please come back—and *do* bring Buddy."

I pulled a really mean trick on one waiter-manager of a restaurant in South Carolina. We had finished our lunch and were having dessert when he came up and informed us that dogs were not permitted in the dining room.

"Do you remove crutches from a crippled man?" I asked.

"Certainly not," he said.

"Then why are you trying to banish my eyes?"

He paid no attention, however, to my explanation that I "saw" only with the help of Buddy.

His accent, during his voluble protests, revealed that although employed in the land of magnolias and spoon bread, he was an Easterner. I decided to fire all my ammunition.

"Well, suh," I drawled in my Tennessee voice, loud enough for everyone in the dining room to hear, "I sho can tell you must be a Yankee. You cain't be from the South. If you were, suh, you'd have a bettah understandin' of Southern hospitality!"

It would have done General Robert E. Lee's heart good to

see that apron-clad enemy in complete rout and hasty retreat, leaving Buddy and me in complete victory on the field of battle.

Whenever Buddy had the chance to "speak for herself," her behavior always opened gates heretofore closed. In one restaurant when the waiter complained vociferously with the "No Dogs Allowed" refrain I so hated, I had him call the proprietor.

We discussed the matter about twenty minutes, during which I almost convinced him that an educated guide dog would raise the tone of his establishment. Finally he said, "All right, all right—go and get the dog. I'll take a look at it!"

I simply raised the table cloth, and there was Buddy, more quiet and composed than many of the other patrons. He was most impressed.

"So my other guests should be so well behaved!" he exclaimed. "The dog, she stays!"

We went there often after that, and every time our new friend bustled over to our table, lifted the table cloth, and gave Buddy an approving pat.

I shall never forget the time we made a dinner engagement with some newly-met, very wealthy people for the purpose of interesting them in the School. We went to quite a nice restaurant, but had not been seated long when the *maître d'hôtel* approached us and apologetically told us he had had a request for us to move.

"If it is convenient for you to cooperate, Mr. Frank," he said, "I will arrange that you have a private dining room at no extra charge."

I put up a big hullaballoo, reminding him that I had been dining there for two years and never had any difficulty about the dog.

His reply was quite startling. "I'm sorry, sir," he said. "It's not Buddy they're objecting to. It makes them feel bad to sit near a blind person."

That one floored me, and I seriously considered withdrawing in favor of Buddy's taking over the fund-raising. She seemed to be knocking down prejudice in her field better than I was in mine.

As commander-in-chief, Mrs. Eustis mapped out a brilliant strategy for winning the battle to permit our dogs to ride in the passenger cars of railway trains. She worked for months to arrange for us to be at a dinner party, just by coincidence, at the same time that General Atterbury, president of the Pennsylvania Railroad, would be present. Naturally there was considerable talk inspired by other guests about Seeing Eye, in which the General showed an encouraging degree of interest.

After dinner, when he was patting Buddy, who had made a beeline to him when coffee was served, Mrs. Eustis joined them.

"You know, General," she said, "these wonderful dogs must stay at the sides of their masters all the time to give them full service."

I must interrupt my story right here to say that the Boss was a very clever woman. She was so smart that just before the crash of 1929, while financial wizards of Wall Street were buying stocks, she was *selling* them and putting her money into government bonds. Yet at the appropriate time and place she could open her big brown eyes and seem the epitome of helpless femininity. When she brought her problems to a great, big strong industrialist, there were very few who passed up the opportunity to prove their superiority by making those little problems disappear.

"We have a perfectly dreadful time," Miss Innocence continued, "with the railroads crating our dogs up in baggage cars."

Buddy, all cooperation, raised her head at the hated words "baggage cars" and gave a low growl.

"I just don't know how to go about getting railway officials to cooperate to let these indispensable, well-behaved companions of the blind ride as passengers instead of packages," the Boss concluded. "Can you help us?"

Five days later her question was answered. She rang me to tell me the good news. "Morris, you can now step on the Pennsy with Buddy like a man, not like a smuggler!"

General Atterbury had just telephoned that he had sent out an order authorizing that Seeing Eye dogs be permitted throughout the entire Pennsylvania system. This was the first road officially to give full "right of way" to our guides.

The very next day Buddy and I boldly and happily boarded the Pennsylvania for New York. We were no sooner seated, Buddy tucked comfortably out of the way underneath my seat, when the conductor told us we would have to get off. "I'm sorry, no dogs are allowed."

"But haven't you heard of the new order to the contrary?"

"Not a word. I wish I could do something about it, but my hands are tied."

"Will you do me a favor and untie them long enough to check on this?"

"Okay, I hope you're right," he said good-naturedly.

He went to the station master, who presumably called the General's office. Just before the train pulled out of the station, the conductor returned in excellent spirits, slapped me on the back, and said, "Son, next time, bring a horse on here if you want to."

After the Pennsylvania gave us the green light, officials of other Eastern lines were more willing to listen. That was all we asked. Buddy herself could usually do the rest.

Through members of the Vanderbilt family, Buddy and I got an appointment to call on executives of the New York Central in their offices at 230 Park Avenue. When I arrived, to my surprise, they did not ask me to board a train and prove that a Seeing Eye dog would not be a nuisance to other passengers. They were so taken with the fact that I had walked all the way from my hotel to their offices alone with Buddy that all they wanted was to see her in action in New York traffic.

"I'd just like to see if she can really go through that bedlam without killing you," one said.

At their request I took the down elevator, crossed Forty-second Street, walked up Fifth Avenue, over to Lexington Avenue, and back to their suite. They followed a little distance behind me.

Only one untoward thing happened. Fascinated at how intelligently Buddy avoided the surging sidewalk crowds, how she paused at curbs until she was sure it was safe to guide me across car-choked streets, a vice-president became so excited that he failed to see a cab make a right-hand turn and he got a fender in his backside. Notwithstanding this attack from the rear, we obtained the permission we hoped for from the New York Central.

Even after this success it was months before we could arrange to see a key man in the railroad industry of the Middle West. Then we reached one of the Van Sweringen brothers in Cleveland. He became so interested in Buddy that he invited the presidents and vice-presidents of eight railroads with which he was associated to come in and see her work. Buddy seemed to sense that this was an important demonstration, and she never did better. Before we left the office, we had hit the jackpot and won consent for guide dogs to ride with their masters on all eight roads. Buddy was very pleased with herself and with the men who had the vision to rescind the discriminatory rule. For their part, one would have thought that these sophisticated tycoons were little boys, they were so delighted when Buddy shook hands all round to show her appreciation.

As Buddy played her part in opening the first railroad, she also helped open the last holdout, the New York, New Haven & Hartford. We were invited to Thanksgiving dinner at a lovely home in Connecticut. A most engaging young lady at my right showed great interest in the story of The Seeing Eye and after dinner simply fell in love with Buddy.

I mentioned our struggle to get Buddy and others like her accepted by the railroads, and she seemed outraged that this particular one was still boycotting these wonderful animals.

"You mean to say Buddy can't travel right along with you?" she asked indignantly. "You mean she has to be tied up six or eight coaches away, as if she would contaminate somebody?"

"It's worse than that," I assured her. "We blind can't even use local and commuting trains, the ones that would do us the most good, because those short-haul lines don't carry baggage cars where they can isolate our dogs."

On the first of January we received notice that really started the New Year right. We were told that the N.Y., N.H. & H. had relented and that the guide dogs could now travel it freely. I called a friend doing public relations for the road and asked him how it happened.

"Remember that nice girl who sat next to you at Thanksgiving dinner?" he replied. "She is the daughter of one of the chief executives of the line. I don't know if it was you or Buddy who gave her a cause, but all through December she gave her father no peace. She pestered him until the twenty-fifth and finally said, 'I will not take a bite of any Christmas dinner in this house until you promise to treat those marvelous dogs like the human beings they are!'"

By 1935, after six years of hard work, Buddy the Pioneer

had completed an important part of her major assignment. She had overcome prejudice and unreasoning resistance to open up new highways for those who could not fight the fight for themselves. Thanks in large part to Buddy, the independent blind could now travel freely anywhere in the United States that an engine and two steel rails could take them.

Chapter 9

━━━━━━━

*P*OURING into our office were applications for far more dogs than we had. Mrs. Eustis, as well as Humphrey, Miss Hutchinson, and I, felt that not every blind person should have one. Some individuals could use them to advantage, others could not. We wanted these rare and valuable guides to go to men and women who would use them to become physically, mentally, and economically independent. Jack expressed our feelings exactly when he said, "This whole process of selecting and training instructors and animals is too expensive and delicate an operation to be wasted on somebody who might turn his dog into a mere pet."

"Or an aid to a beggar's tin cup!" I added.

"Morris," the Boss said, "it's up to you and Buddy to weed out the chaff." So we hit the road again, this time screening candidates.

Among the first we called on was a salesman who could have continued his job in the advertising department of the local newspaper except for one fact—he was enjoying his blindness! He was being taken care of, he did not go out to work, he had his favorite radio programs to listen to, his children waited on him hand and foot.

Here was a delicate case. This man could benefit from a guide dog, and should have one, but not unless he changed his attitude.

When I asked him what he wanted to do, he said, vaguely and unconvincingly, "Earn a living for my family and dedicate my life to helping the blind."

His lofty answer, combined with his demonstrated lack of willingness to pull his share of the load, infuriated me.

"What in the name of the devil had you ever done even to indicate you wanted to dedicate your life to anyone?" I demanded. "You could have carried on, could have sold ad space to bring in a weekly paycheck. That effort would have made you an outstanding community figure. You could have helped every blind person by being self-respecting yourself. Instead, you sit here as if you were paralyzed. You are nothing more than a parasite, making your poor wife, who has plenty to do here at home, go to work to support you."

He was furious, but time proved that my words must have been the shock treatment he needed.

In a few weeks he was accepted for training at Morristown. Upon graduation he told me something I shall never forget. "You know," he said, "after you left my house, I prayed to the Lord for five nights to take you, that you were the meanest, the commonest man I'd ever known. On the sixth night I woke out of a sound sleep, poked my wife in the ribs, and told her, 'My God, what he said was true!'"

That man was a successful person with his dog, his family, and his chosen profession to the day he died. His example of dignified self-help was an inspiration to the blind in his area, even though he never made a formal "dedication" of himself to that cause.

Another man Buddy and I went to see was a Phi Beta Kappa in college but a failure in life. Sitting in his chair, feeling sorry for himself, he had grown fat and lazy. He kept referring to himself as "afflicted." I took this as long as I could, which was not very long, and let him have it.

" 'Afflicted' to me has always signified somebody's being

'teched in the head,'" I told him. "Blindness is merely a handicap. Any good race horse has one, but if he has the stuff, he wins.

"Who in this world," I asked him, "is not handicapped in some way? With some, it may be loss of sight, with others, a defeatist attitude, and the last may be worse off than the first."

Then I took his hand, put it on Buddy's harness, and let her lead him a few steps to give him the feel of it.

I left believing that he would do nothing further to help himself, but some weeks later he came to Morristown. While his spirit of enterprise had atrophied, his mother, I learned, a strong-willed woman who had been his eyes, had her own opened when she saw me put on my hat and coat and walk away with my dog, self-reliant and safe.

Buddy and I found that with the loss of sight came loss of initiative in so many of the applicants we went to see. It was not always easy to speak sharply to people who have more trouble than you might think a human being can bear. It would be easier to minimize their burden instead of saying, as I often did, "Your blindness is like a hand of cards. You've been dealt it; you've got to play it. You can't give it back, so you might as well arrange your suits, organize your thinking, and make the best of it."

I admired tremendously the way one young mother faced her "hand," one of the most difficult that a deck could produce for anyone to be called upon to play.

She was a widow, and was having a real problem with her six-year-old boy, who, naturally, wanted to spend his time with his playmates on the baseball diamond or at the swimming pool.

"Why do you have to be blind and make me lead you everywhere?" he would demand, with a child's cruel directness that went like a knife to her heart.

Here was a candidate that we could really help. She came

to us for her four weeks' training and returned home with a beautiful blonde dog, Lottie.

After about a year I called on her again and found one of the happiest homes I ever entered. She and her son could not have been more close.

On the morning before Johnny's school opened, she took him to his classroom to register. Then she suggested that they celebrate the rest of their last full day's vacation together by going into town for lunch and a movie.

"Gee, Mom," he said as they boarded the bus, "now you're just like other mothers. I'm not taking you around—you're taking me. Do you realize you haven't asked me to run an errand for you in weeks?

"And, Mom," he added proudly, "the other kids wish they had a dog like Lottie."

Not every candidate, I found, was so worthy as that young mother. The Commissioner for the Blind in North Carolina asked me to visit a mountaineer who had been blinded by a bullet. He lived about fifty miles from Asheville. We went as far as a car could take us. Then my driver stopped halfway up the side of a steep hill and said, "There's a cabin, but I don't think your dog can make it through the underbrush on that incline."

"If seeing people make it, Buddy will," I said, and she did.

After I had talked at some length, and in full accent, to the blind man and half a dozen others gathered around a stove in the bare-boarded one room, the woman of the house asked, "Yo' from the South?"

"Yes, Ma'am," I said. "Nashville."

"If we'd knowed that, we'd have give you a hand and showed you an easier way to get here, but me and Pa spotted the Yankee license," she shrugged.

We all laughed, ranging ourselves as allies on the same side of the Mason-Dixon Line.

After that a jug of "corn-squeezin's" was produced, and neighbors began to drop in to see the dog that could guide a blind man through city streets where they themselves feared to go.

My report to the school read: "Recommend candidate be refused. Eyesight lost in shooting fray. Makes living as horse and cattle trader. No ambition to change jobs. Believe candidate capable of selling guide dog if good deal were offered. He does not really need dog; what he needs is mountain goat!"

Word occasionally reached us that one of our graduates was mistreating or neglecting his dog. Naturally we could not allow such foolish conduct to continue. Besides being inhumane, it would reflect discredit on the school and on all guide-dog owners. So Buddy and I investigated each of these reports.

One concerned a burly, middle-aged man who lived in a West Virginia mining town. He towered six feet four inches in height and weighed some 260 pounds, not an ounce of it fat. His tiny wife was only five feet tall. Now I understood the complaints. People had mistaken his heavy voice tone for anger at his Sandy. He had just never tried to curb his giant's attitude toward smaller creatures. He had been throwing his weight around and, to be honest, making a fool of himself. This had disturbed onlookers, but it made no difference at all to Sandy, who was never harmed, was used to his gruff manners, and knew how to handle him.

We talked the situation over and I tried to impress on him the necessity of avoiding even the appearance of ever abusing his dog.

It was a new thought to him, and he was still mulling it over when his dainty little wife took me to the door. Then she told me in a soft, gentle voice, "Mr. Frank, don't you worry. If he ever mistreats that dog, I'll bust a chair over that son of a bitch's head!"

I left with no more concern for the dog. I knew from the

way that little dynamo spoke that she would do exactly what she had promised.

Rumors of abuse were usually due to misunderstanding that arose when someone saw a blind man giving his guide a correction. An intelligent dog, like a bright child, has to be disciplined. Just as surely as it must be immediately encouraged when it does what is right, it must be swiftly rebuked, sometimes with the leash, when it willfully disobeys. After a student goes home with his dog, it takes from six weeks to as many months for them to achieve complete *rapport*. It is something like a marriage; the newlyweds have to learn to understand each other.

We rarely found real mistreatment of a dog. When we did—and that was only twice—the masters, poor devils, had lost their sanity and, as so often happens, had turned against the thing they most loved.

We did frequently find people who were not getting full capacity service from their animal guides. One man let his Peggy take him each morning on a three-mile walk to work in his feed store. She took him along a highway, across several dangerous crossings en route. But, once arrived, she disappeared under the counter and lay there until time to take the master home at night. If he went to the barber shop for a haircut or to the bank to deposit his money, he asked a sighted person to take him.

"Why don't you use Peggy when you run these errands?" I asked him.

"The police chief said it was dangerous," was his reply. His respect for the law had robbed him of the confidence he had brought home from Morristown. Now he received only about 10 per cent of the benefits he could have enjoyed.

I had a talk with the chief and Buddy and I gave him a demonstration. Later on our feed-store graduate wrote me: "Chief Ballard says for me to quit asking my friends to help me around town. He says Buddy convinced him four feet are better than two."

In Indiana we found a wife who was ruining the efficiency of her blind husband's dog simply because she was jealous of the animal. Before getting Diana, he had been on relief; with her, he had become a hosiery salesman, making good money. But he was blind when they married, and the wife liked him that way. She wanted to keep him dependent on her. She wanted to be the important one in his life.

This woman refused to let Diana in the house. "Have that dirty bitch track mud all over my floor? Never!" This separation from her master made the dog feel that he no longer loved her. She lost some of her own affection for him, and her eagerness to serve him diminished.

I am sorry to say that I could not straighten out this situation. The emotional disturbances on all three sides were too deep-rooted for me to dig out. When I left them, the problems of the eternal triangle were still eternal. The wife never let up in her criticism of the "other woman." She was so vituperative about Diana that the poor fellow actually returned his dog to Seeing Eye to board while a psychiatrist attempted to help the wife get her emotions under control.

Buddy and I did not limit our visits to graduates having difficulties. In whatever city we gave a talk, we went to see former students in the area. These visits were marvelously inspiring to me, renewing and strengthening my faith in The Seeing Eye. I knew very well every one of our graduates. I had called on most of them before they came to Morristown and again after they had returned home with their dogs. Almost without exception the change was something thrilling to see. Each in his or her own way developed from a personality blighted from sense of embarrassment or inadequacy to one unfolding like a flower through gaining self-respect.

In a Middle Western town Buddy and I went to see Anne,

who had had Lady for three years. We stayed for hours, and as I left, I asked her to write down for me some of the things we had talked about. This is what she sent me about the change her guide had made in her life.

When my father died, my mother and older sister went to work to support the family. My young brother and I went to the public high school. Everyone was very considerate of me, but it cut me to the quick when, as often happened, I heard myself referred to as "the blind girl." When I went to the store to buy a scarf or a purse I needed, the clerk would always speak to my companion and ask, "Do you think she would like this? Is this what she had in mind?" People treated me as though I were not only blind but also deaf and feeble-minded. I never felt like a complete entity, for all my communication with others was short-circuited by going through a third person.

I wanted a Seeing Eye dog from the time you and Buddy came to our school. I ran my hands over her silky coat and dreamed about the things I would do, the places I would go, when I finally had a beautiful creature like her to lead me.

After getting Lady, I realized that I had not dreamed enough. I had not imagined what she could do for me.

The first revelation of my new status as an individual came by telephone. One morning a saleslady in a local department store called me—*me* personally. "Miss Anne," she said, "we just received a new shipment of dresses and, you know, one of them is of a gorgeous light tan shade that I think will just match Lady!"

That was the beginning of direct communication for me. On streetcars people asked me my dog's name, her age, where I got her, and many other questions that broke through the awkward silence that had imprisoned me so long. At dinner I took my turn like the rest of the family and told what had happened to me during the day. And I told about it in *my* way, for the events had happened to me alone—not to me and a companion.

I enrolled in a typing and dictaphone course at business school. I made my own decision to do this and went alone with Lady to make the arrangements. When I completed the course, she and I made the rounds looking for work. It was hard to convince an employer that I could hold down a job. I finally told the owner of a small manufacturing plant, a Mr. Rogers, that if he would give me a chance, I would work one month without salary; if he did not consider me satisfactory at the end of that time, I would leave.

When the month was up, I couldn't have left if I'd tried. Mr. Rogers came by my desk every morning, not so much to speak to me as to say hello to Lady. She was so good. She stayed under my desk and never got in anyone's way. But she would come out for Mr. Rogers, wag her stubby tail, and put out her paw to say "Good Morning!"

I now had my first real feeling of security. Do you realize what this means to a girl? To go and come as she pleases without fear, to hold down a job and participate in the family support? It rescued me from being the sheltered, handicapped member of the family. Now I was giving as well as receiving.

My first Christmas with my own money I had such fun in the jam-packed stores. Lady would work in and around the other shoppers to get me through the crowds. Often she would nudge someone's leg with her nose and they would automatically make room for her. I was amused to hear one shopper say to her companion, "Follow the redhead with the dog. They'll make a path. That's how I got so much done today. Look, here's my list, almost all checked off!"

I bought all the members of my family the most lavish presents I could afford. They were a double surprise to everyone, for this year Mother had not gone with me to choose for my brother and sister; my sister had not helped me with Mother's. I had shopped alone. I gave my nicest present to Lady, who had done so much for me and changed my life so thrillingly.

A young man, sighted, in my office proposed to me. When I asked him why he wanted to marry me, a blind girl, he said,

"What's the difference between you and anybody else? You can go everywhere and do everything. Besides, I want Lady, and the only way I can get her is to take you both!" So now I am married, entering a new phase of my life, just like any other girl.

When I finished her letter, I thought to myself, "Here is the living spirit of Seeing Eye. Anne is a human being who has dignity and self-respect and the ability to face life courageously and, above all, happily."

A great tragedy is that when blindness strikes, it stops so many mature, intelligent men and women from continuing their work and giving the world the benefit of knowledge it sorely needs. The brain's ability to think is not impaired just because one's eyesight is.

Henry Saunders found that out. He is a brilliant electrical engineer who lost his sight at the age of fifty-four. Believing that he was no longer useful to his company, he retired and resigned himself to a life of inactivity. For two years he did nothing, but idleness, isolation, and helplessness made him so unhappy that he felt he had to do something to save himself from complete degeneration.

He applied to Seeing Eye with some trepidation, because not many people over fifty-five have the physical stamina to stand the strenuous exercise of training. Fortunately he had kept in excellent condition and was equal to it. He returned home with his dog Pal and with new courage.

Saunders and his wife built a house near the campus of a well-known university. Buoyant and vigorous, striding along with Pal, he soon became a familiar figure. He met members of the department of engineering, who recognized his competence and invited him to conduct seminars for graduate students in electrical engineering. This work led to a job as consulting engineer on location for the building of one of the great dams of the West.

His dog restored this gifted man to a life of the mind. Pal gave his master the opportunity to share with others the special knowledge acquired over a lifetime. When I last talked to Henry Saunders at the faculty-club dining room of his university, he patted his dog and said, "Pal has made my last years the happiest of my life."

When I went to see Al Simmons and his dog Jim, I was thrilled to see how some brave souls can adapt to and completely master a situation which would take many right down to the depths of despair.

Al's life without Jim would have been tragic, indeed. Manager of a wholesale coal dock, he was blinded in an accident at fifty-two. Mrs. Simmons was an invalid. Al did the marketing, house cleaning, and cooking.

This evil stroke would have seemed to many the end of the world; and, for all practical purposes, they would have let it be the end. They would have fallen on relatives or charity or, if they could have afforded it, hired someone to nurse them to the last of their days.

Not Al. He got Jim and went back to work. Keen on civil affairs, he was active on many committees, and he promoted the Salvation Army and the Red Cross with special vigor. He became a councilman. Finally he was elected and served for six years as the city's mayor.

Al would not have achieved all this had he not been a man of energy, ideals, and devotion. But neither could he have accomplished it and so led the full rich life he did without the dog which took him everywhere he wanted to go.

Most graduates, of course, simply love their dogs, and affection usually starts very early. A maid at Seeing Eye once reported that the bed of one of the students was not being slept in. I walked upstairs to smoke a cigarette with the boy late one night, have a friendly bull session, and find out what was going on.

When I knocked and asked him if I could come in, I noticed that his answering voice came from the floor.

"What on earth are you doing down there?" I asked.

"I was told that Silver should not be allowed on the bed," he explained, "so I am sleeping on the floor with her!"

A South Carolina boy who had lost his sight in a hunting accident was so fond of his dog that he was convinced that being blind even had some compensations. When I was in Columbia, I tried to get in touch with him. When I telephoned, his mother said he was in one of his college classes and gave me a number to call to reach him. I was amused to find that he was not at the college, where his mother had reported him to be, and more entertained at the telephone conversation I had with him the next morning.

"Well, now, I'll tell you," he said. "Yesterday was such a beautiful day I just felt like going fishing. So I put Barry's harness on and I went, just like I used to when I could see. You have no idea, Morris, what a pleasure it is to play hookey with Barry! Before I had him, I'd join some of the other fellows down at the stream, but when it got to be six o'clock or so, the boys would say 'Come on, time to go home, it's getting dark.'

"That doesn't affect us. Barry knows her way back and the light, or lack of it, doesn't bother me—or the fish. When the sun goes down, Barry just turns over and grunts, as if he's saying, 'Ain't this the life!' If we like, we can just fish right on to midnight."

Most husbands or wives, as one would expect, are grateful for their partner's new freedom and love dearly the dog who brought it.

One day I stopped at the counter of a blind friend of mine who runs a cigar store. He told me he now had a new address.

"We had to move," he said, "because of Pal."

"Was she bothering the neighbors?" I asked, surprised.

"No," he replied. "You see, she took to sleeping in bed between the wife and me, and she was so cute about it we didn't like to stop her."

He paused to wait on a customer, then continued, "It was pretty crowded for the three of us and we didn't have a place for even an extra cot in the room. So—" here he interrupted himself to hand out a package of cigarettes,"—we moved into a larger apartment. Now Pal and I have our bed in the master bedroom and my wife has hers in the adjoining room. We all like it so much better."

I found another dog leading the life of a canine Riley when I went to see a Virginian. His dog, Chief, had no regard for rugs or draperies. He romped all over the couch when I tried to sit on it, nipped my ear, and in general made a complete and thorough nuisance of himself. He was the most spoiled dog I ever saw. I spoke severely to his master for letting him get so out of hand.

"Mr. Frank," he said, "about 200 yards from here is a creek. Some time after I got Chief, my two-year-old grandson, Bobby, visited us. While his mother was upstairs, the baby fell in the creek, face down. Chief sprinted out, grabbed that little boy by the seat of the pants and pulled him to the bank. That dog saved my grandson's life."

He paused for emphasis and then went on. "Mr. Frank," he concluded, feelingly, "it's absolutely none of your damn business *what* that dog does!"

I could understand his attitude perfectly. As a matter of fact, on my travels I found so many dogs who were heroes that I sometimes thought we might as well automatically issue a lifesaver's medal to each one as it graduated from Seeing Eye.

The most touching example I ever encountered of how highly a dog was regarded came to my attention when I went to call on Foster, a man who I could tell was prospering. Six years previously when I had visited him concerning his application to come to Morristown, loose boards creaked on the porch floor as I walked over it, the house was musty, and it did not even have indoor plumbing.

Now, as we drove up, my driver informed me that the fence and bungalow were painted, the porch in perfect repair. Inside, I will admit, that, mountaineer-style, they had a refrigerator in the living room and a bed in the kitchen, but the place was crowded with new electrical appliances and the house smelled fresh and clean as could be.

Foster was out, but his mother told me this story: when she and her husband were married, a well-to-do sister-in-law gave them a very beautiful silver bowl. It was completely out of keeping with their modest income and standard of living. But the silver piece was a lovely thing. She wrapped it up carefully and stored it on the top shelf of her closet. When life was difficult and she needed beauty for her soul's good, she would take it out, polish it lovingly, and put it back.

Then her son went blind. All day long he sat in his room in a chair and did nothing but rock. Back and forth, back and and forth. For two years the house seemed shrouded in darkness. Then Foster got his dog. Thanks to it, her son was up and out every morning, whistling and gay again, earning a good living for them all, loving life. Joy had entered her heart again. Now at last, she said, she had found a fitting use for the precious silver chalice. It was the dog's water bowl.

Chapter 10

$\mathcal{A}$ TRAGEDY in my relationship with Buddy was that, being blind, I naturally could never appreciate fully all that she did for me. Unless a sighted person was there to tell me of her exploits, I was not aware of the spectacular ways she helped me every day. Leading me around yawning holes, awnings, and obstacles that would hurt me, and doing it with such ease and dispatch that I was not even aware of them, was all in the day's work for her.

I got an occasional insight that suggested the magnitude of her service, as the visible part of an iceberg suggests its more important bulk beneath the surface.

For a test, one morning I took my cane and, without Buddy, started to go just one familiar block, the one that took me to the corner drugstore. I discovered more pits, poles, and overhanging tree branches than I dreamed were there, although we made the trip almost every day.

On another occasion, coming from the streetcar toward home, I approached a corner and gave Buddy the command "Left!" To my surprise, she would not turn. She wanted to go straight ahead across the street. Hearing the bark of dogs and the voices of childern playing over there, I assumed that she wanted to go by and let her friends know that she was back from work and would soon be ready to join them for a frolic.

I did not consider it good discipline to let her have her way, so I refused to follow, gave her a stern correction and ordered, "Left!" once more. Again she refused to obey. Thoroughly exasperated by this time, I gave her a piece of my mind. She responded by obediently making a very quick left swing that banged me right into a steamer trunk. Evidently waiting for an express truck, it was sitting right in the middle of the sidewalk—and so was I! Buddy's message could not have been more plain if she had said, "Okay, wise guy. You asked for it. Take the consequences."

One early evening after working hours I felt Buddy slow down to a very cautious pace as we were crossing West End Avenue in Nashville. I followed her with the same discretion that I used in taking cues from her a dozen times a day. Once on the other side I heard a mother say to her little boy, "Look, Danny! Isn't that a smart dog? Did you see how he led his master right over that narrow passage between the open ditch and the water-service truck?"

"I sure did, Mom! It was like an act in the circus! They looked like a couple of tightrope walkers!"

A Washingtonian, a girl, told me an amazing instance of her dog June's quick thinking on her behalf. She was out walking near Dupont Circle when, without any warning, June, in harness, rose on her hind feet, whirled around, and knocked her down.

Some workmen ran to her assistance and told her what had happened. A crane was being moved through the city and a fastening had given way, freeing a giant iron hook. She had been directly in the path of its lethal swinging arc. As it was, the heavy hook had grazed the top of her head. Had it not been for her dog's split-second thought and action, her stroll would have ended tragically.

Needless to say, instruction to meet such unusual situations is given in no dog-training school's curriculum. The knowledge comes, I believe, from the dog's desire to care for his master or mistress, stemming from their mutual love.

I have two good Arkansan friends, "Pinksey" Pinkerton and his wife, Nancy. Jerry, Pinksey's Seeing Eye dog, completes the family. Their married life has always been my ideal of the way two people should get along, so I was terribly shocked to have her tell me, right in front of her husband, "Morris, for the first time since our wedding day fifteen years ago Pinksey yelled at me!"

"Good heavens," I said, "what happened?"

"I had just about finished putting a new coat of wax on the living-room floor. None of it had dried, when I heard the front door slam. It was Pinksey and Jerry coming home. Jerry dashed right out onto my newly waxed floor! 'Jerry,' I shouted, 'keep off my floor!'

"Pinksey shouted right back, 'Don't you dare speak ugly to that dog! He just saved my life!' "

Then Pinksey took up the story. A few minutes earlier he had slipped and fallen while crossing an ice-covered intersection. A car began to bear down on him, its brakes being useless on the slippery pavement. Pinksey, being blind, knew nothing of his danger. But Jerry could see clearly the terrifying situation. He dragged him by the harness handle out of the path of the automobile.

"Pinksey," I said, "what did your wife have to say to that?"

"She sat right down on that freshly waxed floor, called Jerry to her, loved him, and cried."

Death-trap elevator shafts, runaway cranes, and disastrously dangerous icy streets are dramatic examples of the dangers our dogs help us to face. It is in the field of the common garden variety of danger, the menace of traffic, that our dogs perform daily miracles. Carefully computed figures show that more Americans die in automobile accidents than in wars. If those who can see still cannot escape the mechanical murderers, compare the chances of those of us who are blind. It is the Seeing Eye dog that balances the scale against the likelihood of our ending up as one of those traffic fatality statistics.

Forty-third Street in New York is a familiar one to me, and one autumn noon, knowing I had had plenty of experience with that particular hazard, we plunged boldly into it when we got the "go" signal. What I did not know was that, because of detours on adjoining streets, an unprecedented stream of traffic was channeled into Forty-third.

We got halfway across and found ourselves held up by a bumper-to-bumper line of cars rounding the corner and passing right in front of us. Then the light changed. We were really caught, right in the middle of the thickest flow of traffic I ever heard. I was terrified, but Buddy kept her head. She expertly moved forward to let one car pass, then backward to make way for another. Through my fright my mind reached back to my early training for "advice in emergency": "Keep your shoulders square, keep your arms relaxed, follow the dog easily, give her a chance to get across the street."

When we finally made it, I got down on my knees and gave Buddy a big hug and then just stayed there, too weak to move. The cop on the corner came over and said, "My God, I didn't know you were blind. I just thought you were crazy!"

Well, crazy or not, I thought, Buddy and I had battled it out all alone. That taught me. In tight places hold on to my dog. I know I can depend on her. I never know about people.

I had another scare once, crossing Twenty-third Street and Third Avenue. At that time the elevated and the streetcar tracks were still there, and combined to make the very sound of the corner strike terror to a pedestrian's heart. I stepped off the curb and above the pandemonium the shriek of a car's brakes almost split my eardrums. I thought, "This is it!" Black headlines flashed before me: "Fate Catches Up with Morris Frank!"

As I froze, an angry voice right beside me shouted, "You fool cabbie! You almost hit that woman!"

Those screeching brakes were not in my honor at all. I guess that Fate, far from stalking me, was really on my side—and, praise be, so was Buddy.

People were always telling me what close calls I lived through, how near I came to being run down; but I never was even grazed in my whole life with Buddy.

Uncle Willi telephoned me once when I was in Pittsburgh and opened the conversation with "Thank God!" He had just received a message that I had been hit by a trailer, dragged twenty yards, and been badly hurt.

Reports of my death reached me numerous times. I occasionally got lost, bumped a shoulder or stubbed a toe, but I never fell, got hit, or had any reason to criticize my dog's guiding. Buddy's perfect record in this respect was extremely fortunate for the future of The Seeing Eye. Had I been killed while under her care, it would have been not only the end of me but the end of every blind person's chance for freedom through those other wonderful dogs that followed the trail Buddy blazed.

Chapter 11

~~~~~~~~~~

*A*S BUDDY'S fame spread, she became quite a celebrity. Few people in the country would refuse us an interview if we requested it, and some distinguished persons actually asked to be introduced. During one of our stays in Detroit, a very good photograph and write-up appeared in the afternoon paper. Next day we had a gracious note from Henry Ford. "I have often read of Buddy," he said, "and would be glad to meet her if you can spare the time. Would tomorrow at three be convenient? If so, my car will await your pleasure at your hotel."

The great industrialist gave us a warm welcome, ushering us into his office himself, shaking hands with Buddy, and watching our demonstration with genuine interest. Buddy, as usual sensing the atmosphere for her surroundings, assumed an attitude appropriate for the executive suite. She sat very erectly, her back straight as a Prussian soldier's, and her fine head poised and alert. Mr. Ford said with a laugh, "She looks exactly like one of my vice-presidents."

He then invited us to go to Dearborn to visit his famous early American village. Buddy helped me experience it all. When we approached an authentic dwelling, she would lead me to the door and put her nose right under the knob so I could find the latch. The charming tinkle of cascading notes from an antique music box fascinated her; she cocked her head from side to side, listening intently, as if the sad sweet sounds reminded her of the old faraway land of Swiss Vevey she had known long ago. Before we told Mr. Ford good-by, Buddy had her tintype taken. She sat very quietly, seeming to understand that if she moved she would spoil the picture.

Joseph Burns, a good fellow Tennessean who was later Speaker of the House, arranged audiences for Buddy and me with President Coolidge and, later, with President Hoover. Both claimed to be most favorably impressed by her impeccable conduct. Each took the harness, gave her commands, and tested her along the corridors of the White House.

She must have thought that something about carrying on the duties of the Presidency makes a man fall into careless habits, for both these Chief Executives dropped their handkerchiefs and then asked her to retrieve them. Remembering what Buddy had done to mine the last time I tried to show her off, I was fearful for the fate of the C-in-C's "blowers." Fortunately they must have made the gesture seem accidental. Buddy would never have let herself be confused with a trick dog, not even to please the President of the United States.

Once we made such a quick business trip in and out of Washington that we did not have a chance to call on Speaker Burns. He wrote me a chiding letter to Morristown. "I can stand up under the blow of not seeing you, Morris," he wrote, "but the least you could do is send Buddy around."

Newton D. Baker, former Secretary of State, whom we met in Cleveland, completely charmed my canine companion. She kept standing up, putting her head in his lap so he would scratch her ears. He took a fancy to her, too, and the parting was mutual sorrow.

Buddy was very much impressed with Booth Tarkington; nevertheless, with him, as with the other great men she met, she was not awed to the point of subordinating her own personality. Sincerely fond of the author, often at his boathouse in Maine, she would go over, put her head on his knee, and look at him as if asking, "Are you the fine writer who has brought so many people such great pleasure?" And then, while he was drinking his tea and not looking, she would nibble his own graham cracker right out of his hand.

Sitting by a cozy fire at Mr. Tarkington's one autumn afternoon, I dropped a box of matches. Buddy got up from where she had been snoozing, ambled over, picked up the box, and returned it to me. As I patted and thanked her, our host said, "I know it sounds absurd, but something about the way Buddy looked at you when she handed you those matches made me think, 'Why, that dog knows her man is blind.'"

The idea amazed him, as it does many people. We at Seeing Eye, however, have long been completely convinced that it is true. I told him that our trainers often remark that our dogs lying on the floor let the kennel men and other sighted persons walk around them, but get up and move for the blind students. And of course many of my experiences with Buddy showed me that she understood perfectly the special reason she was with me.

Radio raconteur Alec Woollcott was fond of Buddy and she was frequently the heroine in stories that he told over the air. An astonishing coincidence—pure Woollcottiana itself—occurred because of one of his many broadcasts featuring Seeing Eye adventures.

A husky fellow, a driller by trade and father of eight children, was trapped in a plant explosion. He was permanently blinded. For thirty-six hours after they broke the news to him that he would never see again, he lay like a stone on his hospital bed. How could he face life, blind? His mind reeled with frenzied thoughts of self-destruction. But a blind man is helpless even to kill himself, he thought bitterly. How could he do it? Take poison? Who would hand it to him? Leap from a rooftop? How would he find his way up so he could jump? Somehow he must put an end to his life. He was not going to drag on, useless, a millstone around his poor wife's neck.

Suddenly his thoughts were penetrated by a voice which came from a radio on the night table of the next bed. It was Woollcott telling one of his stories of The Seeing Eye.

"Get that, please!" he cried desperately to the patient who was idly turning the dial.

These words, plucked from the air, made the difference between life and death to a man who had already surrendered to despair. Weeks later he walked out of Morristown with his own guide dog, his spirits not only regained but his faith strengthened. A job was waiting for him in the same factory where he had worked before, his wife and children full of love for the husband and father they had almost lost.

"I don't believe that broadcast came from a radio station," he told me. "I'm convinced it was beamed straight to me from heaven!"

Buddy numbered, among her many prominent friends, important figures in the newspaper world. She caught the fancy of many an editor who recognized good human-interest copy when it walked in on its own four feet.

The good will of press and radio people was essential to Seeing Eye's acceptance, and Buddy did her part to win it, always cooperating 100 per cent. She loved to demonstrate her skill at negotiating a difficult street crossing and when it was done would prance around and demand praise for what she very well knew was a first-rate job. Cameramen and reporters liked that.

She enjoyed having her picture taken and always posed enthusiastically. After the snap she would jump up and kiss the cameraman. Many a Hollywood starlet could probably further her career by taking a page from Buddy's book! (And perhaps they do!) At press conferences, if the conversation

142

went too long without Buddy's name being mentioned, she would groan, give a small "yap," yawn, or do something to attract attention. "Don't forget me," was the idea. "You know, one always speaks of 'Buddy' when I'm around."

I am sure her favorite clipping in our scrapbook was the one that appeared in a local paper one December when we went home for Christmas. It was a feature story titled, "Buddy Visits Nashville." The rather long article concluded with, "And her master, Morris Frank, is with her."

Chapter 12

‹‹‹‹‹‹‹‹‹

WHEN Buddy and I had been together about eight years, a growth appeared on the underside of her stomach. By the time of our Christmas visit to Nashville in 1936 it had become quite irritated, and it was obvious that she needed expert medical attention.

She was so much a part of me that I felt I could not depend upon the advice of a veterinarian only. Imagine my relief that her reputation in our home city was such that she was accepted as a patient at Vanderbilt Hospital. There some of the best specialists in the South did not hesitate to examine her. They determined that it was a cancerous condition and should be removed by surgery.

After many frantic phone calls, back and forth, with Morristown we agreed that operating was the only thing to do. Buddy was ten years old. If the cancer were not removed at once, in a few months it might kill her.

Dr. Alfred Blalock, the surgeon now famous for his "blue baby" operation, operated. Dr. Ernest Goodpasture and other well-known physicians were in attendance.

The operation was performed in December, 1936. On that day I waited for Buddy's reappearance from surgery in a state of almost unbearable apprehension. The doctors had neglected to tell me that when she came out from under the morphine, she would throw back her head and howl like a maniac. When she did, this sudden shock felled me as if I had been hit on the head by a hammer. The next thing I was conscious of was a glass at my lips and a nurse saying, "Take this, Mr. Frank, and you'll feel better."

I took Buddy home to a devoted family. No human convalescent ever had more sympathetic care. After all, this creature was even more than the apple of their eyes. She was their son's actual eyes. Everyone vied with the other to see who could give her the most comfort. And all this T.L.C. worked wonders. In a very short time she was herself again, cheerful and apparently rather proud of what she had been through. When company came, she would lie down and roll over, showing off her stitches. Womanlike, she seemed to be saying, "Did I tell you about my operation? My dear, my scar is *that* long!"

For the next two years Buddy continued her full and useful life. We spent every waking moment introducing The Seeing Eye across the length and breadth of America.

At the time she reached her tenth birthday, in October, 1936, she had made literally thousands of friends. On that day Seeing Eye honored her with a celebration in which hundreds joined to wish her many happy returns. The birthday cake was of tasty meat and crunchy dog biscuit, topped by ten candles made of the purest butter. She loved butter, so she very neatly ate these tidbits one by one before she began on her cake.

Later in the afternoon she held court for news reporters and photographers at the George Washington Hotel in downtown New York. Her press conference was a great success and made the front pages of all the papers the next day.

Most of all she enjoyed being guest of honor at the dinner party the Ebelings gave that night. Several of her dog friends were there: the hostess' Putz, Uncle Willi's Beth, Ibbi

Hutchison's Diane and Ellen and Love.

Mrs. Eustis, Gretchen Green, Alec Woollcott, and many other of her noncanine friends came. The Grand Duchess Marie of Rumania, who had already done many excellent camera portraits of Buddy, took one of her best that evening; I still have it on my desk.

For dessert Mrs. Ebeling served ice cream in the form of German shepherd dogs. Alec thought these were in extremely poor taste. Nevertheless he crawled under the table when this course was served and ate his with "the birthday girl." With all the dogs acting like people and the people like dogs, it was a gay celebration.

Though Buddy was far away, she was remembered in Nashville, her "home town." Mayor Hilary House issued a proclamation reviewing Buddy's career. It ended by asking the people of the city "to pause for a moment and do honor to a dog that stands for all that means 'Good Citizenship.' "

Another year passed, and while Buddy still demonstrated her unflagging zeal for her work, her physical strength was not keeping pace with her enthusiasm. Her operation was beginning to take its toll; she slowed down and now definitely showed her age.

While we were on a visit to Nashville about this time, a friend of Mother's reminded her that Buddy was growing old and asked, "How do you know she isn't getting deaf? Or that her own eyes aren't failing? She's dangerous for Morris. He should get a strong young dog, or—mark my words—he'll have an accident."

Mother replied testily, "Surely you remember how Morris was before he got Buddy? Can you ever forget his helplessness and how he resented having to lean on other people? Buddy has given Morris nearly ten years of happiness. I know he'd rather run the risk of a mishap than to hurt her by letting her see him depend on another dog instead of her."

Buddy, who was in the adjoining room with me, and who had also overheard the conversation, seemed to understand. She got up, padded into Mother's room, laid her head on her lap, and licked her hands, as if saying, "You understand, don't you?"

When she was twelve and a half, which is old for a dog, comparing to over eighty for a human being, Buddy was having difficulty getting around, breathing harder and having to rest often. A veterinarian friend of mine advised me to take her to a doctor in Chicago, where we had a talk scheduled.

With some difficulty we found his office on Church Street in Evanston, Illinois. I helped him lift Buddy onto an observation table. He silently examined her for about five minutes, then bluntly announced, "This dog will be dead in three months."

He told me afterward that I turned my artificial eyes straight on him, called him a very ugly name, and fainted. When I came to, I got up, picked up the dog in my arms, and dashed out with her. I clearly remembered the location of the door, the steps, and the place where our driver was waiting with the car. It was as if in the shock my unconscious mind had come to my aid and flashed the directions for me.

Buddy had one more public appearance to make in Chicago before we came home. Though she was sick and weary, when the time came for us to go before the audience, she spruced up, guided me to the platform, and barked at all the proper moments—and at some not so proper.

Afterward she stood quietly so her admirers could pet her. When they had all left the auditorium, this trouper hunched down on her forepaws, tired, old, and worn. That night she could not get up on the bed, so I slept on the floor with her.

Before leaving the city, ill as Buddy was, we called on Mrs. Patrick Valentine, in her office in the Field Building. I reminded her, an old friend of Seeing Eye, how Buddy during her lifetime had helped to open streetcars, bus lines, and railroads to guide dogs from Maine to California.

Now, I explained, although we were allowed on airlines, we always had to ask for special permission, in advance. Before Buddy lay down her pioneering harness, I would like to be able to say that she had made it possible for all guide dogs following her to travel by land and sea and air to lead their blind charges wherever in this wide, wide country they cared or needed to go.

Mrs. Valentine listened silently to my every word. When I had finished, she excused herself for a moment, then returned with, "Will you two come into my son Lester's office?"

We followed her in to find the young executive on the phone. He was talking to the top man at United Airlines. This is what we heard him saying: "I'm sorry, Pat. It just has to be. Mother says she'll never let me inside her house again until it's arranged."

So Buddy and I left for Morristown, the last ride that this gallant personality ever made, not by begging for special permission but by buying a ticket and going on our way like blessedly ordinary passengers. Before she laid down her life, she had completed her job.

United Airlines tipped off the newspapers and wire services that a Seeing Eye dog was taking its first official regular trip by air. When we came down for a stop at Cleveland, reporters and photographers met the plane and asked for pictures.

Buddy did not reveal her illness going down the ramp, because she leaned forward in the harness and I held her up. I did not want it known that she was reaching the end of the road. When the time came to return to our seats, I held back, waiting for the pressmen to leave, because I knew Buddy could not make her way under her own power up that steep gangplank. I would have to carry her and I did not want to hurt her sense of dignity.

I stalled as long as I could, then finally one of the photographers said, "I'd like a shot of her leading you back to the cabin, if you don't mind."

I was licked. I had to confess that Buddy was old and ill and would have to have help getting up the ramp. Immediately several newsmen stepped forward and gently helped me carry her aboard.

And although such a shot might have made them a reputation for sensational human-interest photography, not a single one of those hard-boiled photographers took a picture of Buddy in her time of trouble.

That night we joined the Ebelings for a quiet dinner at Openaka. Buddy, usually so full of vitality and romp, simply flopped down on the living room floor when we arrived. "I have brought him home safely," she seemed to say. "I have finished my journey. I am through." There she lay the entire evening without moving.

We took her some food. She seemed glad to have it and was weakly responsive. We could all see that she was tired, very tired. The end was not far off.

When we returned to our apartment, she seemed glad to be home and threw herself on her bed which we had made for her since it had become so difficult for her to get on mine. In the days following she was as close to me as she could be. She would not go out to take care of herself unless I put the harness on. I felt that she was telling me, "Unless you need me, I'm too weary to go anywhere."

One night I turned on the radio in our apartment and heard news flashes about her illness. When her name was mentioned, she would feebly wag her tail. On one program there was a dramatization of her coming home. It was misleading, because it told about her being put in the kennel to die. This upset me, and she seemed to sense it, because she came over and laid her head on my knee as if to say, "We know the truth, so who cares?"

We did everything to prolong her life and make her comfortable. Our veterinarian and a technician gave her heat and violet-ray treatment for an hour and a half in the morning and again in the afternoon. I couldn't bear to leave her alone, and gave in to her insistence that she come to the office with me. I was really too distracted to do any work, but at least her bed at the office was a change of scene for her. She would lie there and look through the glass partition to watch everything going on. She was responsive and glad to see those who came by to pay their respects.

On the last morning she led me from the apartment to the car. I had to help hold her up with the harness, because she was too weak to stand alone. At the office she would not stay in her place but kept coming over to me. She wanted to be near me all the time, so I took her back and sat on the edge of her bed and stroked her lovely head.

There in the sunshine that streamed in through a window, the gallant creature shivered with cold. We put a blanket around her and I patted her. At last, she reached up, gave my tear-stained face a loving lick, and then dropped to well-earned sleep.

Buddy was honored at her death by more than twenty-seven hundred letters and seven hundred telegrams of tribute from nearly every part of the world.

We laid her to her last rest, wearing her harness and leash, under the three pines on the lawn by the entrance to The Seeing Eye. As I told her, "You're a good girl," for the last time, I realized that my debt to Buddy is greater than I can ever tell. She gave me courage to do things that I would never have attempted had she not come into my life.

Getting married, for example. I would have lacked the nerve to ask a girl to be my wife in my helpless, pre-Buddy state. And I possibly would not have wanted the type of girl who would have accepted. She would almost surely have been the kind to mother me, and that I could not have stood.

The ten years that, thanks to Buddy, I lived as a free and easy, much-traveled, widely-acquainted bachelor strengthened my knowledge that the only type of girl I could fall in love with was one who would recognize my capacity to take care of myself.

One night in Chicago I was going out with a young married couple. "Let's make it a double date," I said. "I know just the one to ask." She was Lois Sellmer Coleman, a very pleasant blonde girl to whom my friend Audrey Hayden had introduced me. She had displayed no protective instincts at all toward me; in fact, she had given back as good as I gave in easy banter.

At seven we were at the Palmer House for dinner and dancing. I soon forgot the other couple completely; all I could think of was the tall, graceful Lois, and how strangely exciting it was to be with her. Every time she laughed, it was a thrill of pleasure for me.

We danced so late that we missed her midnight connection to Glen Ellyn. So, waiting for the milk train, we sat in a Thompson restaurant having flapjacks and coffee and talking away as freely and happily as if we had known each other all our lives.

When I returned to Morristown, I announced to the office, "Folks, I've met the girl I'm going to marry." Lois, of course, knew nothing of my decision.

At my invitation she and her niece, Paula, spent their July vacation at Morristown. I knew that if she and my friends did not click, I might as well forget marriage proposals; The Seeing Eye was my family. After they came to know her, their unanimous opinion was, "Morris, you'll be lucky if that girl will have you."

After Lois returned home, Midwestern Seeing Eye applicants, graduates and anyone else from this area having even remote dealings with our organization got really special service. No business originating within a 100-mile radius of Chicago could be transacted by letter, telegram, or telephone. It required my personal attention. When there was no business, my hobby became riding the day coaches—to Chicago for the weekend, to see the girl I wanted. It took me two years to get her.

A few months after our marriage I learned the hard way that Lois was just the girl I had always looked for, one who made no concessions to my blindness. Leaving the house to go shopping for groceries, she said, "Morris, please scrub the hall and kitchen floor while I'm gone. I put soap and a cloth in the bucket; you can pour the water in yourself."

"What do you mean, honey?" I asked incredulously. "I can't scrub floors. I've never done it before. How can I tell if I get it clean?"

"Listen, Morris. You go all over the country telling blind people that all they need is a dog to be able to do anything anybody else can. So you just try it yourself."

And with that, she left.

With some misgivings about giving up my independence as the master of my household in order to prove my independence as a person, I got down on my knees and tackled the job. I started at the far wall of the kitchen, working down so that I finished by crawling backward out the door. Then I did the same for the entrance foyer.

Lois returned, inspected the hall, and headed for the kitchen. I could picture her standing there, surveying the job.

"Why, Morris," she exclaimed, with surprise and pride in her voice, "the floors are spotless!"

I was as pleased as a pinch hitter who has socked out a homer.

Now I wash dishes, clean windows, and can make a bed with the most proficient "lady of the house." I have never regretted giving up wearing the pants in favor of the apron to do my share of all household chores. I can sometimes get away with a point-blank refusal to do some housekeeping task, but Lois has never allowed me to blame nonaction on blindness.

I can honestly say that after Buddy came with me, blindness prevented me from doing only one thing I really wanted to do—join the U.S. Navy at the outbreak of World War II. But even though I did not get into uniform, I was able to participate.

The Seeing Eye Board of Trustees volunteered aid to the war blinded, free of charge to the government. In Washington, Admiral Ross McIntyre, Surgeon General of the Bureau of Medicine and Surgery of the U.S. Navy, asked me to visit all Navy hospitals and show doctors, nurses, and corpsmen how best to handle newly blinded patients. I received similar assignments from Surgeon General Kirk for U.S. Army Hospitals and from General Hines for the Veterans Hospitals.

Lois and I set out by automobile in October, 1942, to do this job. With us went a new dog who was now being my eyes. I cannot say "was taking Buddy's place," for none could ever do that. A male, he was Buddy II, named to perpetuate the Pioneer's memory. I think Buddy would like that, as well as the fact that the use of her name is reserved for me alone. No other Seeing Eye dog but mine is permitted to bear that honored name.

We began our work in the hospital in Seattle with boys who had been sent in from the South Pacific. Drawing on years of experience in helping the blind adjust to the world about them, we were able to change the habits of the staff who had been waiting on their patients hand and foot. This attentiveness showed good heart but bad practice.

We gave the nurses helpful hints on how to instill confidence in the boys who mistakenly thought that their days of doing for themselves were over. The practical aids we had worked out at Morristown soon had the boys dressing, shaving, and caring for their own needs.

The staff reorganized their outlook and methods. Soon shuffling feet and groping hands were a thing of the past for their blind charges.

The spirit of the patients was marvelous. They responded wholeheartedly to our help and displayed an amazing sense of humor. I showed one young Air Corps Marine, a navigator, how, by attentive listening, he could compensate somewhat for the loss of his sight. "Voice tones," I said, "will help you recognize people around you. And you can find your way to ship's store by following the sound of the jukebox."

"All I have to do is stop, and listen, huh?"

He mulled it over thoughtfully. "Well, Mr. Frank, I may be blind as a bat, but you've reminded me a bat's got the best built-in radar in the world!"

We traveled all over the West Coast giving this kind of instruction, and everywhere received the most cordial welcome.

In one big Naval Air Station hospital in California, I went out to give Buddy a chance to "use the facilities." I had become quite accustomed to soldiers and sailors asking me all kinds of questions about the dog and blindness. On this occasion a man attached himself to me and queried me to the point of exhaustion. It went on for about forty-five minutes. When we were finally ready to return, I turned to him and said, "Well, sailor, I hope you got all the information your little heart desired."

As I entered the main corridor, the executive officer said cheerfully, "I see you had a very long visit with the admiral!"

You would think that should have taught me my lesson, but I learn slowly. Some weeks later, when we had worked our way eastward halfway across the country to a large Army institution, I was setting up my Bell and Howell projector to illustrate a talk I was going to make to the staff. I kept bumping into this fellow. Finally I poked him in the solar plexus with my finger and said, "Friend, get the hell out of the way. The C.O. will be here in a minute and I've got to be ready."

When I finished setting up the equipment, the executive officer whispered, "Good thing you're a civilian. A GI'd be court-martialed for poking a general!"

I found many of the nation's best-known ophthalmologists working in these hospitals, doing a magnificent job. Speaking of them, one who showed me around, said, "Mr. Frank, don't mind if I step away from Buddy—I'm afraid of dogs."

"That's all right," I replied, rather neatly, I thought, "I'm afraid of ophthalmologists."

His answer was quick and to the point. "But Mr. Frank, *I* have never been bitten."

A real challenge to my self-sufficiency occurred when we were just about winding up our tour. We were slowly making our way through a driving rain when we had a blowout. I had often intended to learn how to change a tire but never had. You know what they say about the road to hell.

I got out of the car—no raincoat, I was soaked through practically immediately—and struggled with the hub cap about three quarters of an hour. I finally got it off by losing my temper and yanking it loose. Later I discovered that that is how everybody gets them off.

By a long process of trial and error, I got the new tire on and we continued our journey. At the first filling station I asked an attendant to check it for me. "It's been fifty miles," he said. "It'll stay on."

"Thanks a lot. Fill 'er up, please." Then I said to a second attendant, "And now, as I can't see, will you direct me to the rest room?"

"You changed that tire blind?" he exclaimed. Both of them heaped praise on me until I felt that if I'd had a tail I'd be wagging it furiously. Those two men gave the car such a polishing, inside and out, that Lois said it looked as if it had been through the auto wash.

Our trip took nine months. We had traveled forty-nine thousand miles and visited all ninety-six Army and Navy and all twenty-nine Veterans Hospitals in the United States. I would never have even attempted a project of such scope without the confidence that I developed, years before, through working with Buddy.

When Buddy passed away in 1938, three hundred and fifty dogs were already guiding blind men and women under all conditions, in town and city, farm and factory. All over America they worked—on the West Coast, the Colorado Rockies, on the great plains of Texas, in the deep south of Mississippi, Alabama and Florida, in New England, Maryland, Michigan—everywhere in fact where there were courageous people who wanted to fight back against blindness.

Today the number of guide dog owners has increased to nearly twenty-four hundred, some of which have come back for the second, third, and fourth dog. Some have traveled all the way from Hawaii, Alaska, Puerto Rico, and Canada for their animal companions. They come from all strata of society and return to nearly one hundred different kinds of usefulness. They are newspaper reporters, teachers, lawyers, insurance agents, osteopaths, musicians, factory workers, piano tuners, typists, newsstand operators, clergymen, and social workers. The Seeing Eye work for which Buddy laid the foundation has changed the very lives and spirits of men and women.

I often wonder whether any other dog—or animal of any kind, for that matter—has ever contributed as much to his fellow creature, man, as my lovable companion of ten years. Other dogs have performed courageously as valuable members of police and fire departments, and St. Bernards have done noble work. But Buddy's life affected thousands.

She was a real pioneer, just as surely as those other pioneers who have discovered lands and ideas to the world. She rediscovered the world for the American blind.